$5.00

THE
COLLECTED POEMS
of
OLIVER ST. JOHN
GOGARTY

Prefaced by Wm. Butler Yeats,

Æ, and Horace Reynolds

Oliver Gogarty, Trinity graduate and Dublin physician, has in his time taken part in the Irish Rebellion, served as Irish Senator, written a dozen books, and been friend and counselor to Yeats, AE, Moore, Joyce, and other leaders of the Irish literary scene. He is undoubtedly Ireland's wildest wit and her most accomplished living poet.

It is said that Gogarty might have been very much at home in the 18th Century; his poetry and his wit are in the classic tradition of Dublin rather than of the Gaelic-speaking Irish countryside: The Gaelic meters and rhythms so characteristic of most modern Irish poetry are absent. Present are the irony, sophistication, and bawdy humor characteristic of the drawing rooms of the 1700s, a catholicity of subject matter, and the ever-present evidence of an excellent classical training.

This de-luxe edition of Gogarty's collected poems includes everything that the poet wishes to preserve for posterity from his previously published verse.

OLIVER ST. JOHN GOGARTY. From
a painting by Augustus John.

The Collected Poems

of

OLIVER ST. JOHN GOGARTY

Publishers

THE DEVIN-ADAIR COMPANY

CONTENTS

*A List of the individual poems and an Index of
first lines are given at the end of the book*

The Preface by W. B. Yeats is reprinted from the
Introduction to the *Oxford Book of Modern Verse, 1892-1935*,
by permission of the Oxford Clarendon Press ; and the
Prefaces by A. E. and Horace Reynolds are reprinted
from *Selected Poems of Oliver St. John Gogarty* by permission
of the Macmillan Company of New York.

PREFACE

I

By W. B. YEATS

"TWELVE years ago Oliver Gogarty was captured by his enemies, imprisoned in a deserted house on the edge of the Liffey with every prospect of death. Pleading a natural necessity he got into the garden, plunged under a shower of revolver bullets and as he swam the ice-cold December stream promised it, should it land him in safety, two swans. I was present when he fulfilled that vow.

His poetry fits the incident, a gay, stoical—no, I will not withhold the word—heroic song. Irish by tradition and many ancestors, I love, though I have nothing to offer but the philosophy they deride, swashbucklers, horsemen, swift indifferent men; yet I do not think that is the sole reason, good reason though it is, why I gave him considerable space, and think him one of the great lyric poets of our age."

(From the Introduction to the *Oxford Book of Modern Verse*.)

PREFACE

II

By A. E.

THE POETRY OF MY FRIEND

WHEN I was young I thought of my opposites with terror, but as I grew older I transcended those hatreds, because, I hope, my mood became more spiritual. I came to feel the attraction in opposites, not that I wished to be like them but to understand them, to establish some harmony or balance between them and myself. I found this inclination in others more spiritual than myself. Emerson who could not, I think, have brought his lips to utter a Rabelaisian sentence, does twice in his journal refer almost with envy to the Rabelaisian freedom of speech of the lumbermen. This attraction to opposites may have its roots in a purely spiritual impulse to have life in all fullness, and it may have been the same impulse which made him write to Whitman telling the poet what joy he took in his free and brave thought. I found myself liking Oliver Gogarty when I knew him only as having the wildest wit in Ireland from which nothing in heaven or earth was immune, though often I had reverence for the things he assailed. I never suspected in that rich nature a poet lay hidden, though my intuition should have told me that at the root of all friend-ships and desires are hidden identities. For all his rich vitality the elements obvious in it seemed incongruous with delicate poetry. An athlete in his youth, an airman in later life, his mind thronged with the knowledge and technique of a specialist, his imagination brimful of Rabelaisian fantasy and that wild wit which in every poet but Heine has made timid the sensitive psyche.

All this was not congruous with poetry. But, among the multitudes he contained, there was a poet, a genie in the innermost who gradually emerged in spite of all the dragons in its path. I was astonished when he began to show us verses so finely carved that his genie seemed to have wrought with words as the Image-maker in his own verse treated the hard jade, making a transient beauty into adamant. It is easier to suggest a lovely transience than to carve it in definite forms. Monticelli in the blurred jewelry of his woodland could make glimmer a white arm, a gleaming neck, a gesture, a mothlike flutter of drapery, and leave it to our imagination to create the full riot of lovely life.

But the ideal of Oliver's genie was beauty and mystery achieved by precision. His beauty must shine in the sun not in a shade, and its mystery must be its own perfection. That I think is his genie's true intent in its art; but, when it consorts with the crowd of lusty incompatibles in the house of the soul, it is often deflected and becomes witty with the rest, or it listens to scandal and forgets for a time its own ideal. But I always assume that what is best is most real and I find what is best in lovely poems like *The Plum Tree by the House* in which the genie reveals to the poet the manner of its own artistry, to hold fast to the image, to brood on its beauty until it becomes what it contemplates and is itself a blossoming tree. It is not the secret of such art as I have myself, for my genie would melt all form into bodiless spirit. It looks with wonder on its opposite whose art is to project defined and shapely images and which gets its life from this art. That precise carving in words is in the first poem in this book, where the crab tree grows in the imagination with its stiff, twisted beauty, and, as we read, it becomes as sturdy a dweller in memory as its prototype in earth. Again in the *Coin from Syracuse* how determined the

genie is to miss nothing of the hard drawing of the beauty
it sees until the features

> "Crowned with the thickly rolled
> And corrugated gold"

are built anew in fancy with the curious hands

> "lost
> On the sweet Asian coast"

and then we know at last it was some Irish beauty had
started the genie on its interpretation of the ancient image,
some one

> "Come of the old stock,
> Lords of the limestone rock,
> And acres fit to breed
> Many a likely steed,
> Straight in the back and bone,
> With head high like her own,
> And blood that, tamed and mild,
> Can suddenly grow wild."

When I was young and saw a face that set me dreaming I
tried to track it back to the Pleroma, the fountain of all
beauty, to find justification for my adoration. I had not
then found in Emerson the wisdom which justifies the
image-maker—

> "Tell them, dear, if eyes were made for seeing,
> That beauty is its own excuse for being,"

and I have become less timid and more gallant in my
thought, accepting beauties not in my own hierarchy, and
am happier being able to escape from myself and to see with
the delighted, unfearing eyes of a poet who is my opposite.

Oliver Gogarty has eyes which can see what is most
enchanting and alluring in women. He casts a glamour
over them, the art which Gainsborough had in painting

and which Reynolds, for all his mastery of his craft, had not. How few poets convey to us the enchantment of the women they adored. Their love blurs their art. I doubt if Oliver was in love with any of the women he praises, but, as we read, we feel that we could easily fall in love with the woman he depicts. His cool eye has noticed that second of illumination where the light on limb and dress becomes one with the light in the heart, and he can have no peace until he can give that transience permanence—

> "till the cloud
> Of thought takes definite shape,
> And bodies you forth unbowed,
> Tall, on a bare landscape,
> Where earth the stone upthrusts—
> Holding our exquisite frock
> Against the morning gusts,
> And light is on half the rock."

That is a beauty seen and drawn with precision enough to make it alluring to us. I sometimes think of Herrick after I have read one of Oliver Gogarty's lyrics. The Julia of the English poet is a lovely piece of girlhood. That is much, but she will never be more to our imagination. There is some aristocracy of vision in the Irish poet. He sees the lovely girl, but he suggests, however remotely, the psyche within the flesh. In an instant, she might be transfigured in the imagination and become the dream stuff out of which goddesses, naiads and nymphs were fashioned. That is, the images he depicts, however modern in outward fashion, are still in the divine procession and set us travelling with them to

> "The Perfect, the Forbidden City,
> That's built—Ah, God knows where."

From practice the art of the poet, at first a little stiff, has become supple, and the words will fly up swiftly to catch a sudden glory in their net. This must have come almost as swiftly as the vision it speaks of:

> "I gaze and gaze when I behold
> The meadows springing green and gold.
> I gaze until my mind is naught
> But wonderful and wordless thought!
> Till, suddenly, surpassing wit,
> Spontaneous meadows spring in it:
> And I am but a glass between
> Un-walked in meadows, gold and green."

I take so much pleasure in my friend's poetry because it is the opposite to my own. It gives to me some gay and gallant life which was not in my own birthright. He is never the professional poet made dull by the dignity of recognised genius. He has never made a business of beauty: and, because he is disinterested in his dealings with it, the Muse has gone with him on his walks and revealed to him some airs and graces she kept secret from other lovers who were too shy or too awed by her to laugh and be natural in her presence.

(From *Selected Poems of Oliver St. John Gogarty*.)

PREFACE

III

By HORACE REYNOLDS

GOGARTY IN THE FLESH

I FIRST met Oliver Gogarty in George Moore's *Salve* where he is introduced as Dublin's arch-mocker, the author of the limericks that are on the lips of all Dublin. And in Dublin, most vocal of all cities, where talk is the national art and pastime, it means much to be the crowned arch-ollave of joke and jest. In *Salve* the wicket of Moore's garden clangs, and Gogarty makes his gay entrance fanfared by Moore who cries out in welcome Gogarty's motif, "There was a young man of St. John's," the first line of one of the great limericks, slyly leaving the following lines to our curiosity, and thus confounds the censor, for much of Gogarty's wit necessarily bubbles in secret springs. But he gives complete Gogarty's improvisation on Sir Thornley Stoker, the Dublin surgeon, whose excursions into the suburbs of art were made possible by his skill with the scalpel, his antiquarian touch turning a cancer into a Chippendale sofa or a floating kidney into a Ming Cloisonné. And with the laughter that his sallies arouse in Moore's dinner guests Gogarty fades out of the Trilogy, a beautifully realized minor character.

My curiosity was excited. A. E. and John Eglinton, Moore's other guests, were identifiable, but who was this man whose volatile and grotesque name seemed the mirror of his mind? Like Max Beerbohm in *Enoch Soames* I went

xv

unrewarded to the index of a literary history, Ernest Boyd's *Ireland's Literary Renaissance*, a book that had stood me in good stead in my first flirtings with the literature of the Renaissance. Evidently Boyd in his perhaps too earnest quest for the meaning of Ireland's literature had had no time for personalities: he had been interested only in the written, not the spoken, word. Finally in my copy of *Dana*, a rare early journal, I found printed some of Gogarty's lyrics—the Goddess speaking where the critic was mute—and fresh surprise was added to my already aroused curiosity: this man whose wit was as Gothic as a gargoyle wrote lyrics cool and fresh as a fountain, and as delicate as a beautiful change of light.

Later when *Ulysses* fell into my hands, and it was whispered to me that Gogarty was in it, I recognized him in "stately, plump Buck Mulligan" who comes "from the stairhead bearing a bowl of lather on which a mirror and a razor lay crossed" to open that tragedy of the unconscious, although Gogarty is not plump, and stately, perhaps, only in repose. There in that book without reticences Gogarty piled imagination upon imagination with breath-taking invention, and I knew enough of Joyce's marvellous phonographic ear and photographic eye to know that much of it was but Gogarty printed, and I marvelled anew.

Three years passed, and it so happened that each year I met an Irish poet who had known Gogarty: Joseph Campbell, James Stephens, and Padraic Colum passed in succession through the city in which I lived, and from each I gleaned something of the famous Dublin doctor. To ask of him was to evoke a legend: his name was open sesame to the treasure-house of Gogartiana in which each one who knew him seemed to have a full share. "He does not belong to our spindling, self-nauseated age," cried Campbell; "he is a Buck of the robust, devil-may-care 18th century, born out of time to our delight," Campbell's slower, Northern blood standing momentarily still in homage before the memory of a mind which was lightning. And then to illustrate the quickness of Gogarty's wit he told how as a young poet he had walked down Grafton Street one day, proud of a new, very bright red tie. Suddenly he came face to face with Gogarty. "Tiger! Tiger! burning bright," cried Gogarty instantly, passing on with a swift smile and a bright nod. And I shall never forget Stephens's praise of one of Gogarty's poems, *To a Cock*, in a series of mounting phrases which exploded like a rocket in a vehement "By God, 'tis tragic!" while we all looked at each other in wild surprise. Colum told us of Gogarty's adventures before he had hung up his tankard in stories which ranged from his pilgrimage to the top of the Featherbed Mountain to restore the snakes to Ireland to his offering of the swans to the Liffey, a gesture of gratitude to that river which, when he had been taken out by a group of Republicans to be shot, had offered him the opportunity to escape with his life. We gasped at the audacity of those stories in which man revenges himself on those two great barriers that lie athwart the highway of the mind and keep it active—sex and religion. Our pulses beat to the limericks that immortalize in oral tradition such oddly assorted personalities as the King in Sing a Song of Sixpence; Miss Horniman, patron saint of the Abbey Theatre; and Daniel O'Connell, the Irish patriot. We applauded the skill of the parodies that transubstantiates sound and sense as skilfully as Joyce, with that passion for phonetic waggery which is so large a part of *Ulysses* and the Irish mind, turned *Oliver Gogarty* into *Malachi Mulligan*, keeping the two dancing dactyls and the clash of race and mood in given name and surname. And I shall always remember one occasion in particular which Gogarty ruled superbly by proxy, transforming what might well have been just another dinner into an evening of almost Dublin brilliance. Among others, Colum was there, and Maurice Joy, once secretary to Sir Horace Plunkett, and a friend of Gogarty's youth. Scarcely had we seated our-

selves when someone spoke of Gogarty, and then Colum
and Joy began an antiphony of Gogartian reminiscences;
first one, then the other, would remember one of Gogarty's
limericks, stories, or parodies, and these quotations intoxi-
cated, like a succession of drinks. Then when we were all a
little giddy with excitement and delight, Joy arose to recite
Gogarty's *The Death of Diogenes, the Doctor's Dog*, which is
both a lampoon on the tongue-tied, king-loving Professor
Mahaffy and a parody of Swinburne, written, when Gogarty
was an undergraduate at Trinity, in the quintains that close
the *Atalanta in Calydon*. I can hear Joy now chanting the
lines that Mahaffy speaks over the body of the dog which
had died on the voyage from Greece to Ireland, a hound
especially prized because it had been given him by the niece
of the King of Greece:

> As I wambled awound
>   On the gwound that was Gweece
> I was given that hound
>   By the King's little niece,
> And had rather be fined e'er I found him to gaze
>   on his saddest surcease.

And then the Chorus of Scholars in the house comments
gravely on the action, with a deeper tone, *adagio pesante*:

> He was given that hound
>   By the seed of a King
> For the wisdom profound
>   Of his wide wandering.
> But was it the owner, or donor, or dog that was led
>   by a string?

As Joy spoke the last words of this threnody, I made my
vow. I would make a pilgrimage to Dublin. I had not
seen Shelley plain, but I would at least catch a glimpse of
Gogarty in the flesh!

Two months later I found myself one afternoon before a door in which was set a large silver plate bearing the name *Oliver St. John Gogarty, M.D.* Before ringing the bell, I looked about me. This was a moment of which I had long dreamed; it was not to be hurried over; I wanted to squeeze every possible value out of it, roll it around in the mouth, taste it to the full. At last I was in Ely Place. Across the street was the row of houses, from the windows of one of which, Number 4, George Moore, surrounded by his Monets and Manets and lovingly treading his Aubusson carpet, had looked forth and seen the copy of his masterpiece, *Hail and Farewell*. At the end of the street rose the often spoken of convent wall, for Ely Place is a cul-de-sac; between it and Gogarty's house stretched the sunken garden through the wicket of which Gogarty had first walked into my mind. There was the largest apple tree in all Ireland under which Moore, an Ovid among his friends, had dined; there was the damson tree, "coral boughs in light inurned," of which Gogarty himself was later to sing in one of his most beautiful lyrics.

I rang the bell, I waited, I was ushered into the house, I was conducted to the drawing-room. Dr. Gogarty was engaged with a patient. And as I waited for him, I chatted with Mrs. Gogarty and some company. Mrs. Gogarty politely asked me about my stay in Ireland, and I summarized my trip up from Queenstown by way of Killarney to Dublin, mentioning, apropos of something I have now forgotten, that Muckross Abbey was the most beautiful ruin I had seen in Ireland.

"Ah, you should see ——— ———," said a gay, joyous voice behind me, speaking of a famous Irish woman to whose beauty time has not been kind, and I turned to see coming toward me, eyes laughing, step quick, all smile and gaiety and good spirits, a very young middle-aged man— Oliver St. John Gogarty in the flesh. I knew at once that I should like him much; in fact I already loved him for that entrance, with its flash of the precious power to perceive the hidden nearness of analogies seemingly distant until the imagination has discovered their essential closeness, a power that has given his friends many surprises and much pleasure. It was perfect, that entrance, well worth coming three thousand miles to see and hear.

We admired Gogarty's new Danish furniture purchased in Paris at the recent exhibition. Unlike Sir Thornley Stoker, Gogarty esteems the new, the fresh, the modern. President Cosgrave came in, a quiet, sober man who—unlike most Irishmen—did not want the centre of the stage. He talked little, and, I fear, I listened less. What were presidents to me? I sat finally in the presence of the man who had restored the snakes to Ireland; the author of the great limericks; the creator of that robustious company, Fresh Nelly, Mrs. Mack, Rosalie the Coal-Quay Whore, and the heroic and Rabelaisian Bryan O'Lynn; the cunning maker of the cleverest parody in English literature in which Gogarty flashes back to Keats, "Silent, upon a peak in Darien," "Potent, behind a cart with Mary Ann"—certainly the most joyously witty man in all Europe.

And as if he sensed my three-thousand-mile expectancy, Dr. Gogarty talked brilliantly, telling story after story with the ejaculatory running comment and extemporaneous exegesis of anecdote and phrase which are his habit, as is his raised finger, shaken Puck-like close to the ear. I believe he is the only man in the world who can explain his own jokes and make them funnier thereby, I thought, studying him as he talked.

Youth is the first impression one gets from Gogarty in the flesh—all the Irish seem youthful, but Gogarty is particularly so; youth, and the responsiveness of mind and body that is its privilege. He is a man whose energy makes him restless, whose culture and information are rich and abundant, close to the tip of his tongue, ready for instant mobilization in the face of opening, invitation, or attack.

His is a mind whose surfaces are intensely active, but whose depths are seldom stirred; a fluent, ready mind, flaring up easily into images and analogies, expressing itself from the surface, never pulling an idea up by its roots, never working against resistance; a mind that plays like a fine old violin, from which tone comes singingly.

At seven o'clock the next morning—this in a city where the shops do not open until ten—Gogarty was at the door of my hotel with a small car, and we drove out into the beautiful Dublin hills. The small roadster had no brakes, and we slithered down the steep wet hills around which the road curved in dangerous spirals. Driving under those circumstances would have absorbed all my attention, but not Gogarty's. For him it was only stimulation. All the while Gogarty gave me his memories of the poets, Greek, Latin, Scotch, English, and Irish, reciting whole ballads while we slid over the wet hills, ballads ranging from Robin Hood to an 18th century folk ballad picked up by Joyce in Mabbot Street. Through Powerscourt Demesne we tore, finally coming to a stop in a beautiful quiet glade surrounded by old trees and backed by a high cliff down which a waterfall fell in thin hairs of silver. There we got out. Were Gogarty's spirits quieted by the gentle genius of this place? Not at all. At his command we ran foot races to restore circulation, and Gogarty bested me by no mean margin in the standing broad jump, and he would have easily bested a better man than I. Then back to the car, I breathless, but Gogarty unwinded, and then a drive to the lodge of a house where I was to have luncheon. There he left me exhausted in mind and body, while he, with a gay wave of the hand, sped on his way back to Dublin, as fresh and unwearied as when we had set out five hours before.

The next morning at the same hour Gogarty was again at the door of my hotel; this time we were to go horseback riding. As we rode our cobs slowly through the almost deserted Dublin streets on our way to the Strand, we passed the house where Joyce used to lodge, and the sight of it loosed Gogarty's memories of the author of *Ulysses*. He paid tribute to Joyce's marvellous memory; he spoke of his beautiful tenor voice, even more beautiful than McCormack's; and, of course, of *Ulysses*, which he compared to "an elbow of a broken statue which is the town of Dublin." I remembered that to George Moore Dublin was an old second-hand clothes shop, and suggested that if we combined the two images, clothing one with the other, we'd have a museum scarecrow, a bit of foolish fancy that Gogarty generously rewarded with the high, suspiratory "Lovely!" which is the highest mark of his appreciation.

Soon we were on the Strand and off for a fine gallop around the crescent-shaped beach which fringes the east of Dublin as the mountains fence the west and south. The thunder of eight hoofs on wet sand was as joyous as Gogarty's galloping wit, for unlike Joyce, whose wit depresses and saddens, Gogarty is as exhilarating as a gay band playing spiritedly in four-four time in the morning sunshine. Joyce believes in nothing outside himself; consequently he can never rid self of self; he is devoured by the swarm of his ideas, and yet he feeds on them, and on them alone, and thus the heart-withering circle closes, shutting out the vistas that free man from unhappiness. Gogarty believes in the magnificent adventure of life which, like Taillefer, he charges with ardour, juggling his sword, a feather in his cap, a song on his lips.

And then one week-end we set off to the West. To drive with Gogarty in his small roadster had been a terrifying experience, but when I saw before his door the shell-shaped Mercedes in which we were to make our dash to the West, all yellow hood and mahogany trimmings, shiningly sinister —when I imagined the potential power that now lay quiet under that hood, I shuddered. The John McCormacks stopped in unexpectedly for tea—the tenor, wife, and daughter—and that delayed us, so it was after six when we started.

All my life I had lived in what we think of as a speed-crazed country. I had seen my share of the speed that is born of gasoline and gin, but never had I had such a ride. Gogarty had said, "You'll see the country." Well, I did, in blurs. Getting out of Dublin, the motor coughed and spit. "It doesn't run well under fifty," said Gogarty apologetically; "I have to drive it on the brake." Driving on the brake consisted of seventy to eighty miles an hour down the straightaways of the very narrow, very curving, but very smooth Irish roads; at the curves, foot raised from accelerator, a consequent checking of our terrific speed, an anxious peering around the bend and a prayer that we might not find there in the road before us a peasant and a herd of cows. Then the foot down again on the accelerator, and a resultant surging forward of the long yellow hood into the next straightaway.

And how Gogarty loved it! Leaning his head over so that his mouth might be close to my ear, taking his hand off the wheel to shake his finger coyly past his ear, Gogarty talked.

He remembered his student days at Trinity College, Dublin, under that trio of extraordinary professors, Mahaffy, Tyrrell, and Dowden. He quoted the remark Tyrrell made after Mahaffy had been suspended from preaching in the college chapel for his attempt to exalt the Greek Gods over the Christian: "Since Mahaffy gave up preaching in the chapel, I suffer from insomnia at the services," his mimicry of Tyrrell's high, Oxford-accented voice making the remark much funnier than it is in cold print. He spoke of the many personalities with which Dublin bristled a generation ago, of Zozimus who, with a name like a Renaissance scholar in *us*, walked about Dublin in cricket costume, a strolling satire of the English game; who, although he knew Dublin like a book, insisted on finding his way home by compass. He told of the days when he and Joyce and Trench (Trench is Haines in *Ulysses*) lived together in the Martello tower that Gogarty rented for nine pounds a year. He told of how they objected to a British warship which was anchored off shore so as to interfere with their view, wrote a protest to the British Admiralty, and had the ship removed. And thus passed the lovely fragrant Midlands, Padraic Colum's country, and before I knew it, we drew up before the Spanish Gate in Galway town, our first stop.

From there on the country was lovely, Lough Corrib on our right and straight ahead the beautiful Maumturk Mountains in the closing hour of the long Irish twilight. In an unbelievably short time we drew up at the Leenane Hotel, two hundred-odd miles in little more than two hundred minutes, where I got out of the car feeling as if I had been shot across Ireland on a projectile.

The next day we drove from Leenane through Salruck to a point from which we could see the Mweelrea Mountains across Killary Harbour, where we talked to peasants who looked, as Gogarty said, "not only Pre-Celtic but Pre-Anything." Then back to Leenane and on to Letterfrack where we saw the ruins of Gogarty's old house, now re-risen Phœnix-like as the Renvyle House Hotel from the pile of ashes to which the Republicans reduced it during the Civil War. And if you stay at the Renvyle House Hotel to-day, someone is sure to tell you that it was the former home of a man who is in *Ulysses*. From Renvyle we went on to Loch Tully, where Gogarty has an island on which he was building a new summer place. Although the house was still under construction, Gogarty was already planning how he might alight near it in a seaplane from Dublin.

On our way back from the West we turned south at Galway to visit Kinvarra for a glimpse of the Norman castle Gogarty had bought there with the idea of later restoring it, and our visit surprised an Irish peasant who, to Gogarty's dismay, was stabling his horse in the tower built by the Normans four hundred years before Spenser lived in and absorbed the Irish landscape. When we got out to look inside the tower, Gogarty stopped before it and raised his right hand in the Indian-How-like gesture which he and all Dublin use to signify that what is to follow is a quotation from William Butler Yeats himself. "'The Normans had form, Gogarty, the Normans had form,' were Yeats's words when I showed him my tower," said Gogarty. And then as we walked up the stairs of the tower, its four sides oriented to the four points of the compass, Gogarty spoke of Yeats.

Gogarty is delightful on the subject of Yeats, his attitude toward his famous fellow-townsman being compounded of reverence for his genius, delight in his foibles, gratitude for his kindness, and appreciation of the subtle mummer Yeats can be. Gogarty loves to peer into the folds of Yeats's mind, and he loves particularly to excite him to action. And Yeats, of course, plays up. "I decided to take Yeats swimming," said Gogarty, "but in order to stir Yeats out of dream into action, I must appeal to his imagination. So I talked of the swimming match of Beowulf and Breca; of Swinburne's love of mixing with 'the great sweet mother,' 'Clothed with the green and crowned with the foam'; of Byron's fondness for bathing in the jasper sea. And his imagination thus excited, Yeats reluctantly agreed to go. We got into my car and set off, but as we approached the sea, Yeats's resolution began to weaken:

Yeats (after a mile or two, in a chant-like voice to the accompaniment of faint strains from a psaltery hidden under the hood of the car). Gogarty, I'm afraid I can't go in bathing: I've forgotten to bring a suit.

Gogarty. I thought you would; I have two.

Yeats (after another mile). Gogarty, I'm afraid I can't go bathing: I have forgotten to bring a towel.

Gogarty. I thought you would; I have two.

"When we got to the beach, I gave Yeats a suit and towel, put his pince-nez in my pocket, and we bathed in the jasper sea."

But Gogarty was not so successful in getting Yeats on horseback. "I knew," said Gogarty, "that if I could get Yeats on a horse I could put a new rhythm into English lyric verse." And so he began to speak of the noble and benevolent Marcus Aurelius, who rides in bronze on the Capitoline Hill; of Chiron, wise tutor of Jason and Achilles; and of the Centaurs, who thundered headlong down the roadway of excess—surrounding horseback riding with the tradition that Yeats loves to see about the things he does and thinks of. Again Yeats succumbed, but this time Mrs. Yeats put her foot down. New rhythm or no, she was not going to allow her famous husband to get on a horse.

As we passed through Enfield or Kilcock, I forget which, we were stopped by the sharp whistle of a policeman. We were doing fifty through the village square, but it wasn't for speeding that we had been stopped, primarily. Kevin O'Higgins, Minister of Justice, had been murdered that noon, and the police were questioning all cars. "I am Senator Oliver Gogarty," said Gogarty, mentally assuming the toga; "can I be of help?" He couldn't, and we proceeded on to Dublin.

This past Spring—six years later—I saw him again. He was the same Gogarty, running down the steps of the Statler Hotel to greet me when I came to take him to his Harvard lecture, talking all the way to Cambridge in the automobile, overflowing with anecdote and comment on the life he had encountered in the lecture tour which had taken him from coast to coast, full of fresh thought and fresh enthusiasms. For Gogarty's intellectual capital is in rapid circulation, culture is for him an adventure—the discovery in an obscure Elizabethan poet of the wonderful line, "He grasped at love and filled his arms with bays," the epitome of the life of many a poet; the rescue of some fine ringing sentence with the sound of smitten bronze in it, from a medical treatise; the return to the world of a beautiful old Scotch song, hidden like a violet among the weeds of much that has been deservedly forgotten in an obsolete anthology; the perception in *Old Man River* of a microcosm of life concealed from most of us by the film of familiarity. Of course he had a new story about Yeats; baffled by Mrs. Yeats's watchfulness in his plan to put Yeats upon a horse, he had succeeded in taking him up in his plane, for Gogarty is now a licensed pilot and, the Mercedes garaged, he now wings his way to the West, singing, like the beautiful Swan-Children of Lir. He had taken up A. E., too, but that had necessitated a new safety strap—"the ordinary strap was too small for the God."

Gogarty was, as always, a delight to all who saw and heard him, his modesty endearing him to those who could only partially appreciate his wit, the heaven-sent modesty that goes hand in hand with the shyness with which in his poetry he broods on Beauty, fearful that someone may surprise him on his knees before Her shrine. Almost daily his poetry grows more gay and arch, more musical in its tune, swifter and surer in its choriambic dance, more beautiful in its expression of the delights Nature offers to the inviting eye. Sometimes in his verse that rare marriage of wit and beauty is so perfect as to make us regret all the more the occasions when the wit, laughing, banishes the beauty, bruising a rhythm and breaking a mood that have given us great joy. But gradually, and with all the sureness of Nature, the poet emerges from the chrysalis of the wit. By his poetry will the many of the future know the essence of a personality which, in the flesh, has been the wonder of the few.

(From *Selected Poems of Oliver St. John Gogarty*.)

PRELUDE

THE CASTING

I POUR in the mould of rhyme
  All that my heart would hold:
The transient light on the tower,
  The moat in its wintry gold,
Sunlight, and a passing shower,
  The gleam of your garments' fold
That baffles the eye as you pass,
Formless and lovely things
  Like speech that breaks in a laugh;
To leave them a shape with wings,
  And Time but a cenotaph.
I heat them with more than heat,
  Because they must glow in the cold;
I puddle the white-hot mass,
  And praying with words retold,
To temper Beauty from Time,
  I pour them into the mould.

VERSE

WHAT should we know,
For better or worse,
Of the Long Ago,
Were it not for Verse:

3

Prelude

What ships went down;
What walls were razed;
Who won the crown;
What lads were praised?
A fallen stone,
Or a waste of sands;
And all is known
Of Art-less lands.
But you need not delve
By the sea-side hills
Where the Muse herself
All Time fulfils,
Who cuts with his scythe
All things but hers;
All but the blithe
Hexameters.

ODES AND ADDRESSES

Odes and Addresses

ODE

Written at the request of the Irish Government on the revival of the Tailltean (Irish Olympic) Games

EMPYREAN is the source
Of indomitable will.
God the runner to his course
Holds, and urges on until
Lips and face of blood are drained,
And the fainting limbs are numb:
Till the heart, by God sustained,
Bravely to the end is come.

By the Conflict is revealed
In a runner what is best;
By the struggle in the field,
By the speed which is the test,
By the speed that wears him down
Till the spirit alone can bear
Limbs that stagger for the crown
And the thunder in his ear.

Where are they who ran before
Under Tara's wide-eyed steep;
And the chariots that tore
Parallel the ridges deep?
Where are noble man and horse?
Ah, they both have lost the rein;

They have circled in a course
Tara shall not see again!

Aye, their hands are empty now,
And the green earth clothes their hill:
Gone the glory from the brow
And the sudden shout is still,
Blown upon the wind away
From the land that no man knows,
Folded in the earth are they,
And the grass as freshly grows.

Herald : Silence now and hear the King!

KING LEARY

We are, as our fathers were,
Lovers of the swift and strong,
Lovers of the open air,
Lovers of the horse and song
And the glories of the voice
In the deeds to be retold.
Therefore let us now rejoice
As the kings rejoiced of old.

Room enough for Peace is here
On the green and shaven swards,
For the pitching charioteer,
For the grave contending Bards,
For the young men in the race,
For the stately sport of dames,
For the maidens fair of face.
We have opened Tailltean Games.

Herald : The King of the South. Be listening!

THE KING OF THE SOUTH

King, we have come to this noble place
From the mountainous south of the narrow bays
Where, isled in grass, the short oaks grow,
Their low leaves wet by the tide below,
Where the golden sea-weed is lodged and low
Till the tide returns as smooth and bland
As the tremulous path to Fairyland;
And the moon at night renews the track
With a ladder of light on the waters black:
A misty land that is poor in flocks,
Of tender valleys and heartless rocks,
Of stout lowlanders and, wild without fear,
The deep-breathed runner, the mountaineer.
King, we will try on your plain of Meath
Who may in the running be left to breathe,
As the circling race draws near to its close
And our men, reversing their way with foes,
Fly from each other along the track,
Who may for his running the prize bear back.
Our Bards will sing so the Dead may hear
In their green duns watching from year to year
The Summer come with its grasses tall
And, after a longer interval,
The sweet youth ripen to women and men
To love, to challenge, to glory; and then
The green earth laps them and, all too soon,
They join the watchers within the dun.
We are come, O King, where the games are sped,
To share life's crown with the still-foot Dead.

THE KING OF THE WEST

Where I come from, King, the skies
Are less coloured than the land;

9

And the wildest winds that rise
In their clouds are moist and bland.
If you climbed a mountain peak
When the sun has just gone down,
And the sea's without a break,
Heaven from sea could not be known.

Islands shimmer after dark
Floating in forgotten gold,
Islands reached by no man's barque,
Islands poets' eyes behold.
And I bring my bards to try
Who may conquer in the course
Where the wing's too slow to fly,
Where none may prevail by force.

THE SONG OF THE BARDS

What should follow Sport but Song,
And the victor but renown?
Many men are brave and strong,
But if Courage strive unknown
And no poet make it sweet
With the words that rouse the deed,
Even better were defeat:
Who will men forgotten heed?

We can drive a host that wars
With the long embattled years:
Time gives ground when in the cars
Poets are the charioteers.
Beauty vanishing like Spring
We can rescue and respite,
Raise her from Earth's shadowing
Up into perennial light.

Ode

We can walk the reddened path
In the slippery wake of Conn,
Rouse the Hundred-Battled wrath,
Bid him stay or tarre him on.
We can tell of queenly joy
Underneath the trysting thorn,
And the anger of McRoy
When the wooden sword was worn.

We can sing the noble horse
And the wonder of his race,
Showing how the supernal Force
Turns to Courage, Speed and Grace:
For he sprang from soil and surf
Where the ocean weds the loam;
And he thunders on the turf,
And his speed gives back the foam.

While we hold the Shield of Song
Stands the lineage of Kings;
And our buckler against wrong
Louder than MacNessa's rings.
Loveliness we can renew
Unrestricted by its date,
And the brave man's death undo.
We can bend the neck of Fate.

Now from prairie, hill and bush
Which gigantic rivers drain,
Streams whose single-handed rush,
Like a Chief's, puts back the main,
Comes the old heroic race,
Men whose names are with us still,
And we hail them face to face
In the Games of Strength and Skill.

Where the blue eye beams with light,
Where there is the open hand,
Where the mood is dark and bright
There is also Ireland.
Welcome, Brothers, and well met
In the Land that bids you hail:
Far apart though we be set,
Gael does not forget the Gael.

TO THE MOON

O BORN before our birth began!
Through all your blanched and listening vales,
Far from the echoing shores of man,
Aloof, may sing—what nightingales!

TO THE FIXED STARS

GAZERS at Earth who may not snatch
   A moment's rest, O Sentinels,
Who watch with none to change the watch,
   Is there a Rumour which foretells,

After long vigilance, relief;
   And timeless ease from ageless hours;
A respite from the blaze of Life,
   Deep in a shelter such as ours,

Where you may bathe your eyes in Night,
   Trusting in Death's long "All is well"?
Ah, no! For what can give respite,
   And quench the light perpetual?

Our very shade which seems at rest,
    Spins at the apex of its cone;
The dark in which the stars shine best,
    Is by some solar radiance thrown.

Even the primordial Dark that once
    Engendered light, nor growth debars,
Is phosphorescent with dead suns,
    And pregnant with the dust of stars.

VIRGIL

FROM Mantua's meadows to Imperial Rome
Came Virgil, with the wood-light in his eyes,
Browned by the suns that round his hillside home
Burned on the chestnuts and the ilices.
And these he left, and left the fallows where
The slow streams freshened many a bank of thyme,
To found a city in the Roman air,
And build the epic turrets in a rhyme.
But were the woodland deities forgot,
Pan, Sylvan, and the sister nymphs for whom
He poured his melody the fields along?
They gave him for his faith a happy lot:
The waving of the meadows in his song
And the spontaneous laurel at his tomb.

TO "APHRODITE"

VENUS I called you when our love began:
And I was right; and you Pandemian.

TO LYDIA

WHAT spirit was hoaxed
By your lily-white mesh
From its starry lagoon
On the edge of a cloud
Or the crook of the moon?
What lovely and airy
Capricious and proud
Princess out of faery
Was coaxed and endowed
By the sheath of your flesh
As the moon by a cloud?

As the wing thrills the hand
So your body is thrilled
By this thing from the air
That is held in your glance
And would leap out from there
But that your sweet presence,
So lithe and intense,
Restrains the wild essence
That longs to fly hence
And is but half spilled
To its stars by your glance.

TO NINDE

O YOUNG and lovely! Now I'm left
    With old ideals gone;
Bereft of power to praise, bereft
    Of high comparison.

When Helen first put up her hair,
    She may have looked like you;
Or Dian holding back a tear
    When her first fawn she slew.

14

To Ninde

There's not a limb in Melian land,
    Or veiled by Coan seas,
Which lissom chisel planed; or planned
    By rapt Praxiteles,

To match you from your folded feet
    To little lifted chin,
A line of perfect limbs which meet;
    And not a beam gets in!

But when there is not for the eye
    An equal in the heart,
The outer vision fades; so I,
    To find your counterpart,

Call back the loveliness to aid
    Which stars my world of song:
Ladies whom Time has lovelier made,
    And think of them when young.

But what are planets when the bright
    New crescent, tall and shy,
Tip-toes across the orchard light
    Which tinges half the sky?

FOR A BIRTHDAY

WHEN your Birthday comes, I say:
Happy be this holy day!
Happy may it be for you;
But for me it's blessed too
For the fact that I exist
While you live has made it blest.

Had I lived when Helen shone,
All my days would now be gone.
But I live while you are giving
Joy to all who see you living.
Since my happy lot did fall so,
Lady, 'tis my birthday also.

TO A COCK

WHY do you strut and crow,
And thus all gaudy go
Through squalor, with a show
That tempts derision?
Do you a livery use,
Or dress you up in hues
You were not free to choose
Of your own vision?

Colours of dawn and joy
That with delight destroy;
Your body all a Troy
To house desire,
Your mien as proud and brave
As his who fought to save
The fatal Queen who gave
But gifts of fire.

Strange that a small brown hen
Should charm you thus! For men
Great Beauty shines, as when
The Argive valleys
Bore her limbs for whom Greece
For ten years knew no peace,
Or our own Western seas
Bore Grace O'Malley's.

To a Cock

Their birth no happy star
Attended; rigid war
Beleaguered towns, and far
Deep fields were bloody!
Demure is not the mien
Of Beauty, by her een
The insolent pale Queen
Who makes me ruddy.

What, if I could appear
As you do, and strike fear!
But would she fail to sneer
Who will not heed a
Lover? nor cry "Absurd
You are, but as a bird . . .!
Is it to be inferred
That I am Leda?"

Nor would it much avail
Were I to say "The male
In beauty doth prevail
Largely in Nature,"
For she would but retort,
"Is man the only sort
Whose females must pay court,
My beauteous creature?"

Alas, befeathered bull!
My love's too pitiful,
Too pensive, kind, less full
Than that of bird or
Beast, overcharged with fate
And more compassionate
Than yours you satiate
Half linked to murder.

The more we rise above
The beast or even the dove
Sorrow distempers love;
But yours is gladdest,
Soon gathered and soon spent,
A fierce arbitrament;
And you do not repent
O perfect Sadist!

To Semele none came,
None to each Sabine dame,
Not Hercules aflame—
Not dawn to heaven,
Came with as great affright
As you do burning bright,
Not—for the poor hen's plight—
To Kathleen Kevin;

Further she cannot go,
She falters and lies low
Brought down by love, a throe
That throws us all;
Soon to be scaled and hacked
And, like a city, sacked
With nothing left intact
Within the wall.

When you have persevered
As did the dawn you cheered
When darkness disappeared,
Give not the strife up
Till by the Passion Play
Of Death for Life's relay,
The old authentic way
You conjure life up!

To a Cock

O trample her in dust
So that you slake your lust!
Pull back her neck and thrust
To kill the tempter.
Your peace how dare she fret
With feet demurely set?
Give her another yet
And don't exempt her!

Take vengeance for the sting
In love's elusive wing,
With beak and talon cling
In full refulgence.
O work for all your worth
To bring your spirit to birth;
For this kind goeth forth
By self-indulgence!

For when your spurs were gained
Passion was unrestrained.
Your hues were not obtained
From dust and ashes.
You did of old deride
His spirit who denied.
You are but gratified
By Life's fierce flashes.

Now indignation foams!
The purple of your combs
Is purpler than the plum's
Or purple heather's.
What though it must endure!
Break Beauty! O secure
Some respite from the lure
Of all the feathers!

TO MY FRIEND THE RT. HON. LORCAN
GALERAN
(A GREAT HOUSEHOLDER)

MERIDIAN man, Enstomacher,
For whom the whole world's fruits are fare,
For whom all Life is but a Feast,
And all the world a future Guest!

Spread out the Board, dispense the cost,
There's not a moment to be lost
Until the Mystic Wine and Bread
Are guzzled and engulleted!

Others on canvas spend their soul,
You on the tablecloth and bowl;
And as you fill, proceed to quote
What Shakespeare and Sam Johnson wrote.

We take our seats at your commands,
Upon the fare stretch forth our hands;
And grow amazed, while grows the drinking,
To hear your hobby is clear thinking.

Your table, like a moon silvern,
Shows what a kitchen sun you burn,
An alternating sun that heats
The growing herbs and lowing meats.

O Tableland! O plain of Troy,
Whereon we wage the wars of joy!
You, Agamemnon to our force,
Big-bellied as the Trojan horse!

Well marshalled by your genial roar,
The servants massed in order pour
The blood some thirsty summer shed,
Now ten years rising from the dead.

20

A Great Householder

Still from your cellars' costly glooms
Each bottle like an Orpheus comes,
And bends his golden neck till we
Can all but clasp Eurydice.

A Victory plunges through the air.
As well as Love, wine casts out fear!
The butler's Marathon goes round,
And still your friends orchestral sound.

The artists are in heart to join;
There's scholarship in each sirloin:
"Do you prefer it brown or red?
"What did you say that Shakespeare said?

"The book is somewhere on my shelves:
"Yes; God helps those who help themselves . . .
"Don't mind, my Friend, it's only froth
"I like a dappled tablecloth!

"Wine should not make a man afeared.
"A chewing chin won't spoil your beard.
"Well, let your stomach fight it out,
"Starvation's no soft cure for gout,"

Thanks, thanks! For this (I won't refuse)
Opens the lips of every Muse,
Makes us expand, makes trouble cease
And brings the broad Tiberian peace.

Magee no longer thinks alone,
Clarke talks and rouses silent Hone,
While booming through the mist is heard,
Responsible, the clear-thought word

I cannot move, I will not speak
Without Parnassus' second peak:
The Friend to whom you oft refer,
Your cousin dear and echoer.

Once you fill up the ravening Maw,
There's not a doubt about the Law.
Just cut that chicken through the girth,
I'm battling here for peace on Earth.

But there's a thirst I cannot slake
Till water-lilies drink a lake,
For I must get inside the cup
If I would drink what bears me up.

Once like your Body bulged the Earth,
Pear-shaped, before the Moon had birth.
O keep your tropic waistcoat tight,
Your Belly may fly off to-night!

And, mounted to the heavenly dome,
Another Moon would light us home,
Fair as the ocean shell that rose,
And harvest-full and grandiose!

Born of your bounty, take my Song
Redounding, like a dinner gong,
Translunary recorder pale
Of how your guests you can regale.

Till all the Earth's volcanic heat
Shall bear a better heart to beat,
Fame shall not fail you, generous man,
Magnificent meridian!

TO A FRIEND IN THE COUNTRY

(*Wyckoff, New Jersey*)

You like the country better than the town
And very willingly would dwell therein

To a Friend in the Country

Afar from the intolerable din
That makes New York a barbarous Babylon;
But far more willingly would I be gone
From all this mad bombardment of the brain
To fields where still and comely thoughts may reign
Deep in your stately mansion old and brown,
And coloured like a Springtime copper beech:
My God, I would give anything to reach
Your old house standing in the misty rain,
And turn my thoughts to things that do not pass,
While gazing through a window at the grass
And wet young oak leaves fingering the pane.

TO JAMES STEPHENS

Where are you, Spirit, who could pass into our hearts
    and all
Hearts of little children, hearts of trees and hills, and elves?
Where is the pen that could, sweetly deep and whimsical,
Make old poets sing again far better than themselves?

You passed through all our past worst time, and proved
    yourself no caitiff.
America then listened to a voice too dear for wealth;
Then you went to London, where I fear you have "gone
    native";
Too long in a metropolis will tax a poet's health:

It's not as if you had no wit, and cared for recognition;
A mind that lit the Liffey could emblazon all the Thames,
But we're not ourselves without you, and we long for
    coalition;
Oh, half of Erin's energy! What can have happened, James?

TO A FRIEND

IF it be true that poets, as you say,
Envisage in their verse and populate,
By dreams that shall come true, the future state,
I must be careful whom I shall portray
Lest I sit down, forever and for aye,
With the strange characters I celebrate.
O awful thought: our Fancy is our Fate!
(Let me erase some writings while I may!)
But one thing I am sure of, dear A. E.:
I will confront the malcreated crew,
Victims or merely subjects of my song,
If I can reach the bourne where you shall be
Creating kindness as you always do,
And I may bring my fancy friends along.

TO THE LADY

IN the most intimate years your gables grew
And stood by Oxford on their watery hill;
When all the days were spacious, they were still
A country home of music undisturbed.
You keep your life aloof from common things,
Lovely and strange in beauty of its own;
Like a tall Saint who clasps upon her breast
A Pindar hidden by a palimpsest,
And both ordain a life austere and curbed;
Fixed in the change, and timeless as a shrine
Upon the border of a Grecian town
Where there is calm beyond the reach of gold.
My mind seeks beauty and it dwells on you
Under the elms—and all the air was Spring's,

A leaven of silence in the misty dew
Leavening the light, the shadow leavening,
Your cloak and that tall feather, white under blue—
Walking beside a poet in the evening.

TO A. E. GOING TO AMERICA

DUBLIN transmits you, famous, to the West.
  America shall welcome you, and we,
  Reflected in that mighty glass, shall see,
In full proportion, power at which we guessed:
We live too near the eagle and the nest
  To know the pinion's wide supremacy:
  But yours, of all the wings that crossed the sea,
Carries the wisest heart and gentlest.
  It is not multitudes, but Man's idea
Makes a place famous. Though you now digress,
  Remember to return as, back from Rome,
  Du Bellay journeyed to his Lyrè home;
And Plutarch, willingly, to Chæronea
  Returned, and stayed, lest the poor town be less.

TO W. B. YEATS WHO SAYS THAT HIS CASTLE OF BALLYLEE IS HIS MONUMENT

To stones trust not your monument
To make a living fame endure.
Who built Dun Angus battlement?
O'Flaherty is forgotten in Auchnanure.

And he who told how Troy was sacked
And what men clipt the lovely Burd,
Had seven Mayors to swear, in fact,
Their towns first heard his babbling word.

TO MY PORTRAIT, BY AUGUSTUS JOHN

"O infinite Virtue, comest thou through
The world's great snare uncaught?"

IMAGE of me according to John
   Back from the world behind his brow,
Back from the boulevards of his brain,
   My painted wraith, what ails you now?
Whom have you met with or discerned;
   Where have you bivouacked or lain,
Who look like Caesar late returned
   Exhausted from a long campaign?
Where were the tropic fields you fought?
   What hostels heard your jibes and jests?
Alas! my wraith, you answer not;
   But on your face a pallor rests.
The opals of Elysian skies
   Such as he paints around his friends
Are not reflected in those eyes,
   In vain that coloured peace descends;
And never in the meadows where
   He sets his woman great with child,
And dew has calmed the atmosphere
   And all the willowy light is mild—
O never in his mind's Provence
   Did you come by that look of yours!
Some ecstasy of Love's mischance
   Undreamt of by the Troubadours,
Or message passionate or absurd,
   Has made you look as who should seek,
And yet lose, confidence in a word,
   And seem to think before you speak.
Is it a warning? And, to me,
   Your criticism upon Life?

To My Portrait

If this be caused by Poetry?
   What should a Poet tell his wife?
Whate'er it is, howe'er it came,
   No matter by what devious track
My image journeyed, there is fame
   In that it has come surely back.

TO AUGUSTUS JOHN

These, though my tankard is
   Hung in the pantry
Up like Silenus's,
   And from the chauntry
Only dry memories
   Ring for the Muse:
From my indignities
   Take, and excuse.

WHEN you kept the gears in mesh
Driving on through Lettergesh,
And I kept not very far
Behind you in another car—
Not that I would cast a slur,
No; but accidents occur,
And your driving not your drawing
Was what there might be a flaw in—
Like a God a little cloud
Held you, as with speed endowed
You drove on through the divine
Light of day above the shine
Of the green and grapy sea,
Whose translucent greenery
Broke on crescent sands remote,
Goldener than Helen's throat.

27

For I never see a beach
Sloped within a galley's reach,
But I think of sands afar
And our Lady of the War,

Wondering how many spears
Kept Love faithful for ten years;
And you think me just a fool
Of the sentimental school,
You who revel in the quick
And are Beauty's Bolshevik;
For you know how to undress
And expose her loveliness.

You are right, but am I wrong
To love ladies named in song?
I who feel it like a duty
To love the rare and difficult Beauty
That danger never could forestall,
And towers round about it all.
What better than a far ideal
To help us with the near and real?

Well! you need not rail at me,
For you could not watch the sea,
Nor the purple mountains drawn
Like the neck of . . . .;
Nor the Hawk of Achill strung
Like a cross-bow as he hung
Half invisible in blue;
All these things were lost to you.
For your eyes were strictly glued
On (a Yeatsian rhyme) the road,
And the lake vibrating bright
Just six inches to your right;
And the goats so slow to fly

Till they looked you in the eye;
And the dogs still missed at home
That you "stood no nonsense from";
Geese that never more may tell
Who attempts their citadel—
Geese that fledged Augustus John
Till he seemed to be a swan,
Steering through the clear ozone
For a Leda of his own.
Or a Viking who has steered,
All blue eyes and yellow beard,
To some unawakened isle,
With a reassuring smile;
Or the lion-eyed Sordello
Mountain-met was just his fellow;
Or the gifted Robin Hood,
Driven from his sheltering wood.

Then we spread the things, Ah me!
You but tolerated tea,
And the shallow lucubration
Of a pic-nic conversation;
Till—I hope I don't presume—
Suddenly profoundest gloom
Wrapped you as you gazed apart,
And not one of us had heart
To inquire what was the matter.
So we kept our frantic chatter
Up, to save an awful pause,
Guessing what could be the cause
Of your sudden, silent mood,
What in daylight made you brood.
Could it be that vapour islands
Made an "Evening in the Highlands"
With the mountains in array,
Or recalled "The Stag at Bay"

And the gulf that is betwixt
Those who hunt and hang it fixed?

Did your thoughts' unwelcome pageant
Bring, perchance, your London agent?
With his face and forehead numb,
Eyes like an aquarium?
Not by trifles such as these
Was your heart deprived of ease.

Enough! There is no need to tell
How I broke the gloomy spell,
What I was inspired to give—
By bread alone doth no man live,
And water makes a man depressed:
Maybe silence had been best.

> *When my hawk's soul shall be*
> *With little talk in her,*
> *Trembling, about to flee,*
> *And Father Falconer*
> *Touches her off for me,*
> *And I am gone—*
> *All shall forgotten be*
> *Save for you, John!*

TO THE POET W. B. YEATS, WINNER OF THE NOBEL PRIZE 1924

(To Build a Fountain to Commemorate his Victory)

Now that a town of the North
In which a discerning band
Has caused your name to go forth,
And lifted on high your hand

To the Poet W. B. Yeats

Before all men on the Earth
    As a sign of a contest won;
What should you do with your wealth
    But spill it in water and stone;
With a Dolphin to scatter the spilth,
    To be for a sign when you're gone
That you in the town of your birth
    Laboured and hewed at a cup
To hold what the clear sky spills;
    Why should you not set it up
Under the granitic hills?
    What did the Roman of old,
After the Pyrrhic slaughter,
    But spend the hard-won gold
To bring in the Sabine water?
    Gracious and bountiful men,
Caesars and Cardinals,
    Laid hold of the mountain treasure, and then
Spilt it within the walls,
    For children to dabble and splash,
And break the bead at the brim;
    For sparrows to shudder and wash,
And the Dolphin's freshet unlimn
    The Dolphin under its wave
Till he seem to tumble and reel,
    For his back to a poet he gave,
And he follows at Venus' heel;
    He comes from the depths at a song:
O set him on high in his place;
    For he stands for what flows in the lovely and
        strong
And a sign of the Julian race!

EARTH AND SEA

Earth and Sea

THE FORGE

THE forge is dark
The better to show
The birth of the spark
And the Iron's glow.
The forge is dark
That the smith may know
When to strike the blow
On the luminous arc
As he shapes the shoe.

The bellows blows on the dampened slack,
The coal now glows in the heart of the black.
The smith no longer his arm need raise
To the chain of the bellows that makes the blaze.
I see him search where the blue flames are
In the heart of the fire to find the bar,
With winking grooves from elbow to wrist
As he tightens the tongs in his bawdy fist,
As he hands the bar to his fidgety son
Who holds it well on the anvil down
Till he raises the hammer that stands on its head
And brings it down with a sound like lead,
For fire has muffled the iron's clamour
While his son beats time with a smaller hammer,

And the anvil rings like a pair of bells
In time to the beat that the spark expels,

And I am delighted such sounds are made,
For these are the technical sounds of a trade
Whose glad notes rang in the heavens above
Where a blacksmith slept with the Queen of Love.
The horse is looking without reproof
For the leathery lap that has hugged his hoof:
The patient horse that has cast a shoe;
The horse is looking; and I look too
Through the open door to the cindered pool
That a streamlet leaves where the wheels may cool.
I meditate in the forge light dim
On the will of God in the moving limb,
And I realise that the lift and fall
Of the sledge depends on the Mover of All.

O lend me your sledge for a minute or two,
O smith, I have something profound to do!
I swing it up in the half-lit dark,
And down it comes in a straightening arc
On the anvil now where there's nothing to glow.
What matter? No matter! A blow is a blow!
I swing it up in my bulging fists
To prove that the outside world exists;
That the world exists and is more than naught—
As the pale folk hold—but a form of thought.
You think me mad? but it does me good,
A blow is a measure of hardihood.
I lift the sledge, and I strike again
Bang! for the world inside the brain;
And if there's another of which you have heard
Give me the sledge and I'll strike for a third.

I have frightened the horse, though I meant it not:
(Which proves that he is not a form of my thought).
I shall frighten myself if I ramble on
With philosophy where there is room for none.

The Forge

I was going to say that the blacksmith's blow—
If I were the Master of Those who Know—
Would give me a thesis to demonstrate
That Man may fashion but not create.
He melts the mountains. He turns their lode
Against themselves like a Titan god.
He challenges Time by recording thought,
Time stands; but yet he makes nothing from naught,
He bends Form back to the shapes it wore
Before the dawn of the days of yore;
He bends Form back to the primal state;
He changes all, but he cannot create;
And tamper he cannot with the ways of Fate.
Between ourselves it is just as well,
If Man ruled Fate he would make Life hell.

What have I done?
What shall I do?
                    No wonder Pegasus cast a shoe
When I succumbed to the English curse
Of mixing philosophy up with verse.
I can imagine a poet teaching;
But who can imagine a poet preaching?
Soon I shall hear the blacksmith's scoff:
"The ground is sticky, they can't take off!"
When I press with my thighs and begin to urge
The heavenly horse from the earthly forge.

I know right well that a song should be
Airy and light as the leaf of a tree,
Light as a leaf that lies on the wind,
Or a bird that sings as he sits on the linde,
And shakes the spray when he dives for flight
With bright drops sprinkling the morning light;
For song that is lovely is light and aloof,
As the sparks that fly up from the well-shod hoof.

SUNG IN SPRING

THE gorse is on the granite,
　The light is growing clear,
Our tilted, tacking planet
　Has another course to steer:
Without a wind to fill her
　She can hold upon the tack.
The Captain's lashed the tiller
　So we dance upon the deck.

Some ships go by a motor,
　And some by sails and spars,
But our ship is a rotor
　And she rolls among the stars
And has no fear of crashing:
　Without a spyglass even
You can see the signals flashing
　From the light-houses of Heaven.

Our vessel in her sailing
　Just nods and bowls along,
And half her crew are ailing
　And half are growing strong;
And some make strange grimaces
　At us who dance and shout:
The news from outer spaces
　Depends on who looks out.

Some ships by island spices
　Are scented as they run
Or through ice precipices
　Behold the midnight sun;
And these go home to haven
　For they are trading ships,
But we are touring Heaven
　And we tour in an ellipse.

38

Sung in Spring

We do not fear commotions
    Or anything untoward
From rocks or winds or oceans,
    We have them all on board
With sea-room all prevailing
    For a never-ending trip;
Was there ever such a sailing?
    Was there ever such a ship?

We have not once been harboured
    Since first we left the slips;
We see to port and starboard
    Brave bright companion ships,
And they go with us roundly;
    But we in hammocks rocked
Shall be sleeping very soundly
    Before our ship is docked.

She leaves no wake behind her,
    No foam before her foot
Because the gods designed her
    A rainbow-rolling boat.
We only know she's rolling
    And all the more we sing
Because just now we're bowling
    And rolling into Spring.

No questions can prevail on
    The Master of the Ship;
He won't say why we sail on
    This never-ending trip:
Though young and old and ailing
    Hold contradictory views
I think that simply sailing
    Is the meaning of the cruise.

THE DUBLIN-GALWAY TRAIN

EVERYTHING changes:
Time deranges
Men and women and mountain ranges
Why the Devil can't Time let Well enough alone?
He no longer stoops to set his "*Nil obstat*" on
Trusted, tried and comely things than he seeks to change,
Wither, age and alter them and the best derange.
This has happened just of late to the Galway train
That with passengers and freight crossed the central plain
Pulling out from Dublin town that Liffey's stream divides
West to old grey Galway town where Corrib meets the
    tides.
It strains at first, then settles down and smoothly rolls
    along
Past villages with Gaelic names that sweeten on the
    tongue:
Clonsilla, Lucan and Maynooth beside the long canal
Where yellow-centred lilies float and no one comes at all,
The long canal that idle lies from Dublin to Athlone,
To Luan's Ford: but no one knows who may have been
    Luan,
The Royal Canal that joins two towns and makes of him
    a dunce
Who holds that nothing can be found in two places at once:
A long clear lane of water clean by flags and rushes rimmed,
Where, crimson-striped, the roaches steer, and, by the lilies
    dimmed,
The greenish pikes suspended lurk with fins that hardly stir
Until the Galways train comes on and shakes each ambusher.
The lovely hills are left behind; but soon the rising sun
Will overtop the mountain range and make the shadows run.
The light that flushes the hills was low;
But now it gathers to overflow

And shadow each bush on the central plain
And gather the dews and catch the train.
And light the steam
In its morning beam
Making a fugitive rainbow gleam.
Past walled Maynooth
Where they teach the Truth
In the meadow called after Druidical Nooth.
Puff, puff!
That's the stuff
As if there weren't white clouds enough!

Like a charging knight with his plumes astream
The train comes on with its sunlit steam,
Past fields where cows are chewing the cud
To Mullingar where the Square Mill stood,
Where the cattle-dealers with rough red skins
And gaiters buttoned across their shins
Wait for another train; they wait
For cattle-drovers to load the freight
Of blunt-nosed cattle with tousled coats
Bound for the East and the English boats:
Cattle-dealers replete with knowledge
That is not taught in an English college.
It blows
And goes,
A whale that feels
The pistons stabbing its driving wheels.

It reaches Moate where a king lies still
Under the weight of a man-made hill.
On and on, until, quite soon,
It will come to the ford that was held by Luan,
Where, as in Spenser's pageantry,
The Shannon "spreading like a sea"

41

Flows brightly on like a chain of lakes
Or linkèd shields that the morning takes:
The lordly stream that protected well,
When jar-nosed Cromwell sent "to hell,"
The Irish nobles who stood to fight
That Bible-bellowing hypocrite.

From the bridge you can see the white boats moored,
And the strong, round castle that holds the ford.
Over the bridge it slowly comes,
The bridge held up on its strong white drums,
To enter Connaught.   And now, Goodbye
To matters of fact and Reality.
Ballinasloe where the hostings were,
Ballinasloe of the great horse fair
That gathers in horses from Galway and Clare,
Wherever the fields of limestone are:
Mayo and Boyle and Coolavin
Between the miles of rushes and whin
And mountains high in a purple haze,
Streams and lakes and countless bays
Of Connemara where still live on
The seaside heirs of the Sons of Conn.
Then Athenry where the kings passed by
From whom was named the Ath-na-Righ.
It rests for a moment at Oranmore,
A square grey castle protects the shore.
The Great Shore, limit of Galway Bay;
And Galway is only six miles away!

The engine-driver can wipe the oil
From his forehead and hands,
For his well done toil
Is over now; and the engine stands
Only a foot from the buffer-stop
(He eased her down till he pulled her up).

The Dublin-Galway Train

Oh, see the children jump about
As doors are opened and friends come out
With paper parcels.   What endless joys
Are hidden within those parcels of toys!
The county ladies in English tweeds,
With leathern faces fox-hunting breeds,
And shoes that give them a look of men,
Have come to the station "just to look in."
But never an officer home on leave
Is seen; instead, they only perceive
The rakel, card-playing boys debouch
And pay up their losses with search and grouch.
Oh, what a wonderful Noah's ark!
Lady Phillipa of Merlin Park,
Holding her parasol half up the handle,
Is back from Daly's of Dunsandle.
Where gold-headed Daly delights the gazers
As he leads the field of his Galway Blazers.
The Station Master opens a door
And clears a passage for Morty Mor,
For Morty Mor is known to own
The principal works of Galway town.
He is not one of the county set,
(Though he helps them out when they lose a bet)
His saw-mills hum and he sells cement,
Potash and lime to his heart's content.
The workers he sacks on Saturday night
Are back on Monday morn contrite;
In spite of his temper, deep at the core
The heart's all right in Morty Mor.
That little boy lost is found again;
He ran away to the end of the train,
For all he can taste in his youthful hour
Of splendour and terror and speed and power:
The harnessed hates of water and flame,
The engine brings with its seething steam.

43

Earth and Sea

The platform now is empty again;
And empty stands the Galway train.
(Strange that nobody came to call
On the lonely men in the urinal.)
Land that is loved in ballad and song,
Land where the twilight lingers long,
May you be crossed and crossed again,
Forgetting the bus and the aeroplane,
By nothing worse than the Galway train.
Who shall tell how, when I'm dead and gone,
Gaily the Galway train came on?
How it puffed with pride on a road of its own;
How it whistled, *Waeshael*! to each nearing town;
How brightly its brass and its copper shone?
It seemed to be painted to match the scene
Of boglands brown and the trees between
With its coaches brown and its engine green.
It brought the towns where it stopped good luck,
Goods, the result of a bargain struck;
And it never ran over a cow or a duck.

Now all is changed for an overplus
Of passengers packed in a reasty bus,
A crowd that stinks and the air befouls,
And children pewk as the full bus rolls:
(A popular government plays to the masses
And that's what they get who abolish the classes)
Lady Phillipa whose share of charity
Fails when it comes to familiarity,
Lady Phillipa, her feelings hurt
Because Democracy means such dirt,
Is sitting, a most disdainful rider,
With the man from her gate-lodge sitting beside her.
The Law of Change would be just a jest
Were we sure that all change were a change for the
        best.

44

JUST ONE GLIMPSE

IT makes me sadder day by day
To think the streets won't pass away
And all the houses in between
Lift like a transformation scene
That would, for just one glimpse, disclose
The windy oak, the wilding rose,
Rocks, and the springs that gushed before
The streets connected slum and store.

THE BLACKBIRD IN THE TOWN

The music Finn loved was that which brought joy to the heart and light to the
countenance, the music of the blackbird of Letter Lee

HERE behind the huddled houses
Which the squalid gardens break
Golden bill my heart arouses
With his golden gurgling beak;
Disregarding all the squalor
In a backyard after rain
Boldly lifts the Bird of Valour
His mellifluous refrain:
Lifts the fanfare heroes hearkened
When his singing shook the dew
In the dells by oak-leaves darkened
Eighteen hundred years ago,
Sings the song to which Finn listened
When he first was famed and named,
And the ruffian blue eyes glistened
For Finn loved the bird untamed.
I too hear the self-same whistle
Purling all around his nest

Sin_ing to the eggs that nestle
Underneath a browner breast,
Hear the wordless notes transcendent
Over every human rhyme,
Careless, sweet and independent
Of all circumstance of Time;
And I think: though many wrongs ache
In my heart, what matters wrong,
If I sing but for the Song's sake,
If I reach as brave a song,
Filled with fight and self-reliance
Warring with all evil chance,
Loudly whistling my defiance
In the slums of circumstance,
Or, above all, go one better
And, ignoring human wrong,
Bravely as the Bird of Letter
Fling on air a heartless song.

IN THE GARDEN

Pink and white apple blossoms suddenly appearing
Making April lovely after a late Spring,
Constellating the air of morning with their beauty,
Crowding and populating empty invisible spaces
Long before the leaf, their coverlet of green:
Clarions of the world's unborn beautiful faces,
Reminders of the exquisite loveliness that has been.

Perfect beautiful momentary blossoms,
I who am momentary cannot long endure
The tension of your beauty, the knowledge that embraces
Beauty yet to come, Beauty gone before;
The uninterruptible implacable procession

Of Beauty moving onwards from the Fountain to the
    Bourne.
Therefore I take comfort and walk for a few paces:
So I go where Beauty goes, I care not to return.

IF SIGHT WERE SOUND

IF sight were sound,
O the blazon of the gorse bush
Calling from the granite where the heavy air is scented,
Challenging the Summer with its golden clarion;
And how can Summer answer, the Summer silken tented,
Drowsed by Paynim perfumes in its blue pavilion?

If sight were sound, you could hear the blossoms tinkle
Tinkle on the tree tops popping into sight;
And, on the ground, you could hear the periwinkle
Ringing all its faery bells along the leafy light.

If sight were sound,
O the stillness of well-water
Waiting for the blessing of the crozier-holding fern!
The crystal, cold limpidity
Like silence in Eternity,
Like silence when the strings are hushed before the notes
    return.

If sight were sound,
O the northern Aurora,
Thrilling in the zenith like the song of all the stars!
Ah, could we hear, that song were unsustainable;
Sight is better soundless while the weighted spirit hears.

But sight and sound are mingled in the water's
Lovely lymph that wavers as it sings and rolls along
To form a pool wherein
Reflected lean the willows
Bending heads to listen to the sky's stilled song.

THE CRAB TREE

HERE is the crab tree,
Firm and erect,
In spite of the thin soil,
In spite of neglect.
The twisted root grapples
For sap with the rock,
And draws the hard juice
To the succulent top:
Here are wild apples,
Here's a tart crop!

No outlandish grafting
That ever grew soft
In a sweet air of Persia,
Or safe Roman croft;
Unsheltered by steading,
Rock-rooted and grown,
A great tree of Erin,
It stands up alone,
A forest tree spreading
Where forests are gone.

Of all who pass by it
How few in it see
A westering remnant
Of days when Lough Neagh
Flowed up the long dingles
Its blossom had lit,
Old days of glory
Time cannot repeat;
And therefore it mingles
The bitter and sweet.

It takes from the West Wind
The thrust of the main;
It makes from the tension
Of sky and of plain,
Of what clay enacted,
Of living alarm,
A vitalised symbol
Of earth and of storm,
Of Chaos contracted
To intricate form.

Unbreakable wrestler!
What sapling or herb
Has core of such sweetness
And fruit so acerb?
So grim a transmitter
Of life through mishap,
That one wonders whether
If that in the sap,
Is sweet or is bitter
Which makes it stand up.

TO THE LIFFEY WITH THE SWANS

KEEP you these calm and lovely things,
    And float them on your clearest water;
For one would not disgrace a King's
    Transformed, beloved and buoyant daughter.

And with her goes this sprightly swan,
    A bird of more than royal feather,
With alban beauty clothed upon:
    O keep them fair and well together!

As fair as was that doubled Bird,
  By love of Leda so besotten,
'That she was all with wonder stirred,
  And the Twin Sportsmen were begotten!

THE WATER LILY

BETWEEN two elements you float,
O white and golden melilote,
Emerging by a Cyprian birth
The loveliest flower assoiled of earth!
You float, becalming leaves between,
Like sunborn patines turned to green,
Where, by the lake's tree-sheltered shores,
Stem-anchored floats a fleet of flowers.
I fold the oars along the boat
To lean and, like you, dream and float.

The windy mountains, ledge on ledge,
Neighbour your lake by ocean's edge;
And breakers crash not far beyond,
Yet nothing moves the quiet pond
Whereon you float like some unheard,
Ineffable and perfect word,
As if the lake's still spirit drew
Out of the depths to bloom in you,
And gather all that depths may tell
Into one perfect syllable.

There is no sound. Your golden glow—
A sky above, a sky below—
Is now the centre of a sphere;
All else is waived nor enters here;
Nothing offends the fairest bud
That lifts from immemorial mud

Its parted lips as if to say:
"There is no dubious mystery,
No answer and no antidote:
Between two worlds I bloom and float."

THE DRAGON FLY

OFTENTIMES I wish that I
Were a glancing dragon fly:
That this bulk of bone and brawn
Instantly were off and gone
And I dancing on a beam
By a spring or little stream
Iridescent, shining bright
As if, by some blessèd sleight,
Somebody had knotted light:
Swift and instantaneous
As if there were two of us
At the same time here and there,
Faster poised than piercing air;
Symbolising, as it were,
In instantaneity,
Slumbers an eternity.

For my colours I would use
All the rainbow's middle hues,
Stilled with speed or brightly flashing
Like a bubble; or a splashing
Dewdrop shaken from the trees
By a wing in Paradise;
While, below, the stream or spring
Kept the bright air shimmering:

Happy and ephemeral
With no Autumn touch at all:
Just a swift ephemeris
Fashioned to keep up with bliss,
Dancing off without decay:
A moment! And then, gone away!
Proof there lies, instinct in slime,
Time's swift triumph over Time.

LIFFEY BRIDGE

I GAZED along the waters at the West,
Watching the low sky colour into flame,
Until each narrowing steeple I could name
Grew dark as the far vapours, and my breast
With silence like a sorrow was possessed.
And men as moving shadows went and came.
The smoke that stained the sunset seemed like shame,
Or lust, or some great evil unexpressed.
Then with a longing for the taintless air,
I called that desolation back again,
Which reigned when Liffey's widening banks were bare:
Before Ben Edair gazed upon the Dane,
Before the Hurdle Ford, and long before
Finn drowned the young men by its meadowy shore.

THE PLUM TREE BY THE HOUSE

IN morning light my damson showed
Its airy branches oversnowed
On all their quickening fronds,
That tingled where the early sun

Was flowing soft as silence on
Palm trees by coral ponds.
Out of the dark of sleep I come
To find the clay break into bloom,
The black boughs all in white!
I said, I must stand still and watch
This glory, strive no more to match
With similes things fair.
I am not fit to conjure up
A bird that's white enough to hop
Unstained in such a tree;
Nor crest him with the bloom to come
In purple glory on the plum.
Leave me alone with my delight
To store up joy against the night,
This moment leave to me!
Why should a poet strain his head
To make his mind a marriage bed;
Shall Beauty cease to bear?
There must be things which never shall
Be matched or made symmetrical
On Earth or in the Air;
Branches that Chinese draughtsmen drew,
Which none may find an equal to,
Unless he enter there
Where none may live—and more's the pity!—
The Perfect, The Forbidden City,
That's built—Ah, God knows where!
Then leave me while I have the light
To fill my mind with growths of white,
Think of them longer than
Their budding hour, their springing day,
Until my mind is more than May;
And, maybe, I shall plan
To make them yet break out like this
And blossom where their image is,

More lasting and more deep
Than coral boughs in light inurned,
When they are to the earth returned;
And I am turned to sleep.

THE ETERNAL RECURRENCE

I THANK the gods who gave to me
The yearly privilege to see,
Under the orchards' galaxy,
April reveal her new-drenched skin;
And for the timeless touch within
Whereby I recognise my kin.

SUBURBAN SPRING

Now the delicious air
Persuades the lovely trees
To loose their golden hair
From old embroideries
And make an airy screen
Of gold that turns to green.

Delightful it is now
To see the crooked bough,
The crooked bough that dapples
The ground beneath the apples,
Look pink and fresh: as brave
As many a straighter stave
Or willow that, by sleight,
Makes drooping a delight.
Cherries in bloom spring up
As high as the house top.

Suburban Spring

And all the air is filled
With sprays suddenly stilled;
A soft, green, maple rain
Has paved the little lane,
The lane beside the rill
That runs down to the mill;
And every little gully
Gushes, replenished fully;
And in the fields beyond
The ducks upon the pond
Are dipping, scooting, ducking;
Foals, calves and lambs are sucking,
(A thing I would not mention
But for pastoral convention)
And Peggy's out, not caring
To ask how Dick is faring:
The Miller, where no breeze is
(It's dust or sinus) sneezes;
And men in sleeveless shirts
Are plying little squirts,
Or making rainbow mists
With a kind of hose that twists;
And all the world's agog
Like a seedsman's catalogue:
I know that Spring has come;
But not how, or wherefrom.
I would have been a fool
Had I not gone to school
To find out what brings on
This blithe phenomenon.
The teacher said, The sap
Is, once a year, on tap;
And, also, that we roll
Each day around the Pole;
And that these brave things come
Because it's out of plomb.

PERENNIAL

THE other day I chanced to see
By an old lot a cherry tree,
An old wild cherry blooming brightly,
A sight of joy in the unsightly.
It sprayed the air with April snow
As merrily as long ago
When every little wind that blew
Could bend it, and with blossoms strew
The garden or the shaven lawn.
The lot was bare, the house was gone;
And yet the brave old tree bloomed on.

Bravo! I cried. You make me think
Of some old Roman soused in drink
His wreath awry upon his head,
For all that, primely chapleted;
Or that gowned man who loved to foster
My waking wits, *Tyrrellus noster.*
I like the rings upon your rind
Suggesting hoops. They bring to mind
Barrels and kilderkins enough
To stillion the Septembral stuff.
How do you keep your sap so young?
If I could only break in song
As you in bloom, and disregard
Ruin around this old back yard,
I'd raise such foison of sweet sound
That trees would jig it on the ground;
Kettles and garbage cans would swirl:
You'd think that Orpheus found his girl;
Or that this old daft heart of mine
Improved, as it grew old, like wine.
I feel the soul within me sing:
By God, I'm grateful for the Spring

That makes all fading seem illusion;
The foam, the fullness, the profusion;
For every lovely thing misplaced;
The bloom, the brightness and the waste!

THRUSH IN ASH

BARE above the hedge, already
Thick with leaf, the leafless ash
Stands, resisting still the heady
Spring's excited sudden flash;
Like a deep reluctant lover
Whose still heart is slow to love,
But the more it takes to move her,
When she loves the more she'll . . . Hush!
Coloured like his branchy cover,
Ash-eye speckled sits a thrush.
Lack of shelter little daunts him:
If the branches lack their green,
All the better may the mountains
Through the leafless boughs be seen.
You may count up five, or count tens
In between his fangled notes,
While the evening smooths the mountains
And on silence music floats:
Sweetly sudden knots in silence
Like the way a violet shows,
Interrupting green with sweetness,
Presently its purple glows
Like a drop of nectar taken
From the cup that Hebe spilt;
Dew fallen down from Ida, shaken
When great Hera kicked the quilt.

Lightly from the boughs ungreening
Floats the light and lyric cheer,
Just a voice that takes a meaning
From the place and those that hear.
And the silence feeds his whistling
As the evening lights the stars,
Or my ear my fancy, listening
To his interrupted bars.
O my fancy stop your straining
After subtile simile;
Listen to the curled flakes raining
From the song-bird in his tree;
Cease to taint with mortal dreaming
Such a liquid lovely song;
Now the evening air is creaming,
And the hills are smooth and long!
Like the mountains which the Magi
Seek beyond the starlit road
When the Tuscan mixes magic
On the painted oaken board,
And you see smooth light pervade all
Trees transfigured, leaves unstirred,
And the mountains to a cradle
Dwindle, cradling the Word.
Here the ash tree with a trellis
Of its young boughs yet unblurred
Screens the golden dusty valleys
Stilled to hear the singing bird.
Music: silence: silence aching,
Till the few notes twisted clear,
Lovely thoughtless music making,
Lancinate the inmost ear;
Exquisitely thin and sweeter
Than the high sharp sickle moon,
Perfect, being incompleter
Than a promise past and blown,

Sounds that cease before enticing
Thoughts and fetters of the word;
Here is Sound for Song sufficing,
Leafless ash and singing bird.

THE OAK WOOD

You could not see a linnet's wing
Between the oaks that wait for Spring,
Because the air is green and dim
With mosses on each bole and limb.

But soon they'll tingle in the blue
And all their amber joy renew;
And transubstantiate to wood
The Spring's impalpable blue blood.

And they will drain, ere time be past,
From Beauty gall to make them last
To gaze on many a festive sight:
The wedded heir, the ruddy light.

THE APPLE TREE

Let there be Light!
In pink and white
The apple tree blooms for our delight.
In pink and white,
Its shout unheard,
The Logos itself, the Creative Word,
Bursts from nothing; and all is stirred.
It blooms and blows and shrivels to fall

Down on the earth in a pink-white pall,
Withered? But look at each little green ball,
Crowned like a globe in the hand of God,
Each little globe on a shortening rod;
Soon to be rosy and well bestowed,
A cosmos now where the blossoms glowed
Constellated around the tree,
A cone that lifts to infinity.
Each rosy globe is as red as Mars;
And all the tree is a branch of stars.
What can we say but, "Glory be!"
When God breaks out in an apple tree?

LULLABY

LOLL under pines where, faint and far,
The coast is like a scimitar,
So faint and so far down below
The blue in silence turns to snow.

Or call the spendthrift Summer up
When squandered is the buttercup,
And watch the purple pomp unrolled
On every acre's Cloth of Gold;
And hear again the drowsy hum
As drunken bees go barging home.

Or watch the pane that glimmers through,
When twilight makes the valley blue,
With yellow. light to find its match
In one big star beyond the thatch,
And all the air's a mild alloy;
Of grief that's half akin to Joy.

Lullaby

If thoughts of Love be kept afar—
For Love can waken more than War,
Whose greatest captains could sleep sound
Before the fatal final round—

Sweet Sleep, the whole world's treasure trove,
The crown and only cure for Love,
Will come, and gently lead your soul,
So when it leaves the Will's control,
It may not on the fruitless coast
Of Waking Dreams be starved and lost.

ANGELS

In an old court-yard,
Seen from a lane-way,
Down by the Liffey,
Somewhere in Dublin,
Whitened with stone-dust
Dwells an Italian;
And he makes angels.

There are too many
Makers of tomb-stones
Whitened and formally
Carven with crosses,
Dwelling among us:
But he makes angels
Down by the Liffey.

Now I remember
Pagan Pompeii
With its black frescoes
Brightened by Cupids,
Flying attendants,
Winged amorini,
Angels of Venus.

Aye; and I think of
Hermes the Angel,
After his flight from
Crystal Olympus,
Skimming and fanning
With his winged sandals
The violet water;
And in the four-fountained,
Wonderful island,
His thankless reception.

Backwards and forwards
To Middle Ages
Lightly my thought goes
Thinking of Dante
Drawing an angel;
And the tip-pointed
Wings of some airy
Angelic chorus.

What does the poor dusty,
Dublin Italian
Know of the grandeur
Of his great nation?
Grim civilisers,
Law-givers, road-makers,
Founders of cities,
Dreamers of angels,

Far from the sunlight,
Far from the citron,
White, with its branches
Over white tables
Lighted with red wine,
Under grape trellises,

Angels

Here in a lane-way,
True to his nature,
Making an angel?

O for ten thousand
Gifted Italians
Dwelling amongst us
Just to put angels
On the black fresco
Of this most dismal,
Reasty and sunless
Town where the meiny
Of Heaven's chief subjects,
The Christ-beloved children
Are housed in a horrible
Graveyard of houses!

I am a lover
Of Beauty and Splendour,
Lover of Swiftness,
Lover of Brightness,
Lover of sunlight
And the delightful
Movement of water,
Starving in Dublin
For Beauty and Brightness,
Starving for gladness:

God send an angel!
Not a mere figment
From childhood remembered,
God, but a far-flashing
Terrible creature,
An awful tomb-shattering
Burning Idea
Of Beauty and Splendour,
A winged Resurrector,

One with a message
To make the announcement:

Not in His Death,
But in Christ's resurrection
Lieth salvation.

Break down the tenement
Walls that surround them;
Lead out from festering
Lane and back garden
The Heirs to the Kingdom,
To sunlight, to highland,
To winds blowing over
Green fields; and restore to
The sons of a City,
By seafarers founded,
The sight of white clouds on
An open horizon.

Raise up a man—
What though he must shout from
The mountebank platform
To gain him a hearing—
With knowledge, with vision
And sense of the grandeur
Of human existence,
To plan out a city
As grand, if not grander,
Than Georgian Dublin,
With broadways and side-walks
And dwellings proportioned
To what in the nation
Is faithful and noble;
To save this old town
From the artisan artist,
The cottage replacing

Angels

The four-storey mansion,
The cynical largesse
Of hospital-builders;
And all its bad conscience.

Build up with gladness
The house individual
Set in its garden,
Detached and uncrowded;
So that the children
In health grow to greatness;
The family hold to
Its proper distinction;
So that the nation
Be saved from soul-slaughter,
The living damnation,
Which comes from the crowding
That leads to the Commune.

Build not in lanes
Where the thought of an angel
Is one with a tombstone;
But out where Raheny
Gives on to Howth Head
And the winds from Portmarnock;
Or build where Dundrum,
With its foot set in granite,
Begins the long climb
To the hill which O'Donnell
Crossed ages ago
In his flight from the city.
Why should the sons
Of the Gael and the Norseman
Be huddled and cramped
With broad acres about them
And lightning-foot cars

At their beck to transport them,
Which overcome space
Like the sandals of Hermes?

Nations are judged
By their capital cities;
And we by the way
That we fashion an angel.

SONG

MADE BY SIR DINADAN FOR SIR TRISTRAM
THAT AN HARPER MIGHT PLAY IT
BEFORE KING MARK

Incipit citharista

Two trees grew in a garden close.
    Cock a doodle doo! And who goes there?
These young leaves were fresher than those
    For those were withered and warped with care ;
As the sap runs in the root of the wood
A tree doth wax in his lustihood
Till buds be thickened and leaves protrude;
    And sappy Spring is happy.

There was a nest in the elder tree.
    Cock a doodle doo! And who goes there?
A song bird's home in the leaves to be;
    But these were withered and warped with care.
A cuckoo sat in the leaves and trolled:
Cuckoo. Cuckoo. Look who look old.
Cuckoo, Cuckoo, Cuckoo, Cuckold!
    And sappy Spring is happy.

Hic calcibus citharistam ejiciunt.

DUNSANY CASTLE

THE twin dunes rise before it, and beneath
Their tree-dark summits the Skene river flows,
An old divine earth exaltation glows
About it, though no longer battles breathe.
For Time puts all men's swords in his red sheath,
And softlier now the air from Tara blows;
Thus in the royalest ground that Ireland knows
Stands your sheer house in immemorial Meath.

It stands for actions done and days endured;
Old causes God, in guiding Time, espoused,
Who never brooks the undeserving long.
I found there pleasant chambers filled with song,
(And never were the Muses better housed)
Repose and dignity and Fame assured.

CROKER OF BALLINAGARDE

BALLINAGARDE was a house to be sure
With windows that went from the ceiling to flure,
And fish in the river and hens in the yard
And Croker was master of Ballinagarde.

There were mares in the meadows: the grass was so good
That cows never tired of chewing the cud;
One mouthful sufficed all the sheep on the sward;
They forced them to fatten at Ballinagarde.

So close and convenient and wide were his grounds
He could hunt with the Tipps or the Waterford hounds;
And many's the cup and the Horse Show award
That shone on the sideboard in Ballinagarde.

He bought his own whiskey and brewed his own ale
That foamed up like beastings that thicken the pail.
No fiddler no more nor the man with his card
Was ever sent empty from Ballinagarde.

His daughter got married at sweet twenty-two:
To lose her was more than her father could do.
To give her away it had gone very hard,
You could tell that by Croker of Ballinagarde.

The wedding was over a week and a day
Before the last guest could be driven away;
For everyone's going he tried to retard:
"What ails ye?" said Croker of Ballinagarde.

One day when out hunting and going like fire
His horse was flung down—Oh, bad scrant to the wire!
And something in Croker was broken or marred,
So the parson was sent for to Ballinagarde.

The parson remarked as the grounds he druv through
"The land's in good heart.   What a beautiful view!
It's but what I'm thinking 'twill go very hard
To comfort the owner of Ballinagarde."

He tried to persuade him and make him resigned,
On Heavenly mansions to fasten his mind.
"There's a Land that is Fairer than this," he declared.
"I doubt it!" said Croker of Ballinagarde.

NEW BRIDGE

New Bridge is the oldest bridge
    The Liffey passes through.
There must have been an older bridge
    When this new bridge was new.

New Bridge

But, new or old, the water flows
    In many a gleaming stage
As careless as a thing which goes
    And is exempt from age.

So pleasant is it on this bank,
    I often wonder why
They set the piers out rank on rank
    And raised the arches high.
They must, deluded by a dream,
    Have thought, as I have done:
The other side of any stream
    Is better than your own.

The water bends and thickens as
    It rushes at an arch.
The piers like soldiers in a pass
    Stand halted on the march.
The hissing stream escapes to fall
    In mocking undertones.
But would it be a stream at all,
    Without the bridge and stones?

They built as men built who believed
    In Life that lasts forever.
And hardly were those souls deceived
    Who bridged the clear black river?
The soul survived, as any dunce
    Can prove: for it is plain
That that which gets in trouble once,
    Shall troubled be again.

I'd rather hear these arches praised
    Than arches anywhere.
Not that the Eternal City raised
    To Settimo Severe;

Nor those that leave the walls therefrom
 To tap the Sabine ridge,
Can match these arches here at home
 In Liffey's oldest bridge.

The black bright water over there
 Is flaked beside the brink,
As if the stallions of Kildare
 Had bent their necks to drink.
And underneath an arch I see
 A long grey gleaming reach,
Half shadowed by a breeze, maybe,
 Or, maybe, by a beech.

The long grey lines of steel are gone
 Which crossed here long ago:
The colours, the caparison,
 All gone; and I would go
But that I fear I might repent
 My going, if I found
The side from which I willing went
 Looked better from beyond.

GLENASMOLE

Do you remember that thrush in Glenasmole
In the high lane on the West side where I made the engine stop,
When he perched across the roadway like a fellow taking
 toll:
So well within his rights was he, he would not even hop?

That thrush is the owner of all Glenasmole,
From the mild bends of the river to the purple-stemmed
 rose bushes;
For the men who had the giving of such things when Life
 was whole
Called Glenasmole, as it is still, The Valley of the Thrushes.

Glenasmole

There is not one of all the throng of giant men surviving,
The men who dwelt with magic, apple-cheeked and steady
    eyed;
But the thrush whose happy armour was their love of Song
    is living
And he sings the song unaltered that he sang before they
    died.

Strong is the delicate line of generations:
Two thousand songs unbroken of the thrushes in the Glen.
Two thousand years cannot restore the mighty exultations
Of men whose manhood now would be incredible to men.

Song under leaf by the water in the valley!
Bird's throat distended! For the men of old who died
Left a fame beyond all language in the music of their ally,
In the throbbing song outshaken of the bird with bosom
    pied.

There beyond the river and the ridge is Bohernabreena,
The Road House by the road that runs beside a vanished inn;
I can see it like a window opened clearly in the saga
Of an ancient battle ambush that no chivalry could win.

When the Lochlann galleys raided and consumed the kingly
    hostel
Where the chieftains sat in silence with their spears in water
    cooled,
What happened? O what happened? Can the soft notes
    of the throstle
Tell how the golden heroes in their chivalry were fooled?

Far though they are, forget not that the bushes,
The wild rose with its dull white thorns, the hedges and
    the stream
Are nearer to our longing in the Valley of the Thrushes
Than any glen in any hills that neighbour near to dream:

Wings that fly low for a moment in the twilight;
Kings undisturbed by the blaze and battle roll;
Bloom in the seed; the song in egg; the grey light
That holds so deep a glory in the Vale of Glenasmole!

LIMESTONE AND WATER

This is the rock whose colours range
　　From bright to dark when wet with rain,
Clear as an eye whose colours change
　　From smoke-grey blue to dark again:
This is the limestone base of earth
From which the best things come to birth.

And the stream shallows where its walls'
　　Smooth steep, which ivy pennons coat,
Down from bare earth abruptly falls,
　　And stands as if it stood in a moat;
Above, a sapling shows its root:
The wild stream darkens the cliff foot.

Out of this rock the stone was smashed
　　That gave long beauty time to grow;
The hammers rang, the chisels flashed:
　　It answered back with fire the blow;
And it gave gifts and guards enough
From limestone to the Parian stuff.

Water and rock by warriors wed
　　Here with the landscape well accord.
They built beyond Time's ambuscade,
　　Builders and wielders of chisel and sword.
So well they dealt with stone and stream
Eternity deals well with them.

And where the grey sky turns to white,
 Failing the limits of the land's
Far-shining girdle, dark, upright,
 The strong four-cornered tower stands;
And nearer, where the grey sky lowers,
The long green tunnels close on towers.

And here where Time has trampled down
 The white-thorn bush and blurred the track,
Up stands the steep unblunted stone
 And brings the lance-straight ladies back,
And lights again those eyes of theirs
As brave as glints from young men's spears.

For not a thing that ever grew
 To win Time's heart can Time forget:
With clouds he blends the lichens' hue;
 The mountains with the parapet;
And crowns that tower's denizen
Who had more than her share of men.

Wherever Life is made secure
 Beauty is gardened to become
As lovely as its walls are sure
 Foundations fit for Beauty's home.
And like long reaches, stilled by weirs,
So Loveliness wastes not with years.

The castle by the shallow ford:
 In ruin, but the upright line
Above the tangle keeps its word:
 In death the unbroken discipline!
And O, what great well-being went
To build the enduring battlement!

ANACHRONISM

TALL and great-bearded: black and white,
The deep-eyed beggar gazed about,
For all his weight of years, upright;
He woke the morning with a shout,
One shout, one note, one rolling word;
But in my dreaming ears I heard
The sea-filled rhythm roll again,
And saw long-vanished boys and men
With eager faces ranged around
A dark man in a market place,
Singing to men of his own race,
With long blithe ripples in the sound,
Of isles enchanted, love and wrath,
And of Achilles' deadly path;
The great ash spear he used to fling;
The bow one man alone could string;
Odysseus in the sea immersed
Who never heard of "Safety First,"
Nor went to a Peace Conference:
For Homer was a man of sense,
And knew right well the only themes
Of Song, when men have time for dreams.
And then, indignant, down the lane
The great dark beggar roared again.

SUB ILICE

WHO will come with me to Italy in April?
Italy in April! The cherries on the hill!
The sudden gush of rivers where the valleys rib the mountains;
The blue green mists, the silence which the mountain valleys fill!

Is that Alba Longa? Yes; and there's Soracte.
Soracte? Yes; in Horace: don't you "vides ut," you fool?
No! She's not a model . . . you will have her husband
    on us. . . . !
Though her buttocks are far better than the Seven Hills
    of Rome!

Cherries ripe and mountains! Young wives with the gait of
Goddesses; and feelings which you try in vain to say
To the gay vivacious calculating native;
If you knew Italian you would give the show away.

What is the attraction?   Why are we delighted
When we meet the natives of a race that's not our own?
Is that which we like in them our ignorance about them;
And we feel so much the better where we know we are
    not known?

Well, it does not matter.   I am thinking of a stone-pine
Where an Empress had her villa on the great Flaminian
    Way;
And the blond Teutonic students who have come so far
    for knowledge,
And the fräuleins who come with them on a reading holiday.

If I met a tall fair student girl from Dresden,
Whiter than a cream cheese, credulous, and O
Earnest, and so grateful for the things that I might teach her,
And I took her touring, would she have the sense to go?

I would through a ringlet, whisper . . . "This is Virgil's
Confiscated farmstead which his friend in Rome restored.
The Mastersinging races from the North came down here
    merging;
And your hair was heir to colour that great Titian preferred.

How my pulses leap up! I can hardly curb them,
Visiting the places which a poet loved . . . Ah, well!
Never fear the nightfall. . . . Veniemus urbem!
My friend can take our taxi and go look for an hotel."

Here between the last wave of the hills subsiding
And the river-beeches which are growing bald with age,
Gentle as the land's rise, lofty and abiding,
Rhythm's mountain ranges rose to sunshine from his page.

" 'Is this Virgil's birthplace?' " Scholars are uncertain—
You cannot be a scholar if a thing is too well known—
There's the Idylls "ilex: if we use it for a curtain,
You can sit on half my raincoat and my half will be a throne.

Virgil was Menalcas: let me call you Phyllis.
Now look up the Idyll where they tried what each could do:
There! 'Vis ergo inter nos,' and 'turn about's,' 'vicissim';
My pipe though not wax-jointed yet can play a tune or two."

*   *   *

Friends, you must forgive me for this utter nonsense.
To-day I saw an ilex where the Dodder streels along;
And that togaed exile made me so despondent
That I called the light and glory which it shadows into song.

Thwart in the world I control are many seasons,
Many climes and characters obedient to a spell;
I turn to human grandeur's most exalted voice for reasons,
And not the least, that Virgil led a soul estranged from Hell.

OUGHTERARD

Do ye know Oughterard with the stream running through
    it;
The bridge that falls down on one.side like a hill;
The trees and the pleasant, respectable houses;
The white waterfall and the old ruinèd mill?

76

Oughterard

God be with the night when I drank there wid Sweeney
Till he brought the "special" from under the floor
And dawn came in square through the bar-parlour window;
And "Jaze us!" Sez Sweeney "It's twenty past four!"

In old Oughterard I could get on quite nicely,
For there I know decent, remarkable men:
Jim Sweeney, the Sergeant and Fr. McNulty
Who took the first prize with his running dog "Finn."

Bad cess to the seas and bad cess to the causeways
That keep me from goin' back homeward once more
To lean on the bridge and gaze down at the goslings,
And get a "Good morrow" from black Morty Mor.

CONNEMARA

WEST of the Shannon may be said
Whatever comes into your head;
But you can do, and chance your luck,
Whatever you like West of the Suck.

There's something sleeping in my breast
That wakens only in the West;
There's something in the core of me
That needs the West to set it free.

And I can see that river flow
Beside the town of Ballinasloe
To bound a country that is worth
The half of Heaven, the whole of Earth.

It opens out above the town
To make an island of its own;
And in between its sky-blue arms
The grass is green as any farm's.

77

Earth and Sea

As often as I take the road
Beyond the Suck, I wish to God
That it were but a one-way track
Which I might take and not come back.

The very light above the bay,
The mountains leaping far away,
Are hands that wave through homely air,
To make me shout "I'll soon be there!"

It is not everyone gets on
Where dwell the Seaside Sons of Conn;
It is not everyone that's wanted
Where things are apt to be enchanted:

Where you may see if you look out
The hills and clouds tumbling about;
But suddenly the fun may stop
Until they find to what you're up.

You are supposed to understand
What brings the sea so far inland;
And why the water-lilies be
Close to the gold weed of the sea.

You must not ask what kind of light
Was in the valleys half the night,
Now that you are beyond Beyonds
Where night and day were tied by bonds.

And if you see with half an eye
Two lovers meet, O pass them by!
Remember that the Others do
As you have done by them to you.

And never ask the rights or wrongs
When mountains shake with battle-songs;
Because the Fight surpasses far
The things which merely lead to war.

The light is thronged as is the dark;
But here the wise make no remark:
For if it comes to comments on
The glory, then the prime is gone.

The lanes that end on hill or strand
Of this, the Many Coloured Land,
Are dearer than the burdened roads
That cross the Lands of Many Loads.

It's here that I get out to walk;
The Shannon's there for you that talk;
But I can only work my will
Where mountains leap and clouds lie still.

DAWN IN VERMONT

THE sun is rising mistily,
   The valley fills with gold.
I lie and wonder sleepily
   How many suns of old
Arose and filled the valleys
   And lit each tree from tree
Along the forest alleys
   And not a soul to see!

HIGH ABOVE OHIO

LIKE a timeless god of old
With one glance I can behold
East and West and men between
On the pleasant mortal scene.

Earth and Sea

Looking at them from above
I can see them as they move,
I can tell where they will go,
Where they're coming from I know.

I who with a single glance
See them going and advance
Can perceive where they are winning,
See the End in the Beginning;

See alternate valleys gleam
Each one with its little stream,
And the undulant, immense,
Free, American expanse;

See the rivers on the plain
Break to catch the light again;
And the towns and villages
Islanded by fields and trees;

And I make a little prayer
As I see the people there,
For I have not quite forgot
That I share the mortal lot.

God, on Whom Time never bears
Disregard not mortal years,
For a year to men may be
Precious as eternity.

Look on men in thorpe and town
Walled between the Dawn and Down
And remember that their cares
Overbalance pleasant years.

Think, when looking through the clouds
At their little streams and woods,
Streams and woods to earthly eyes
May present a paradise.

Leave them happy on the earth,
Relative to death and birth
Till, in peace, their minds transcend
The Beginning and the End.

NYMPHIS ET FONTIBUS

SOLDIER of Rome, well-trained and hard,
Who dwelt in Britain once and warred,
With no outlandish creed to mar
The stern salvation of the war.

Strong in yourself, you bore your care,
Your soul was like your camp, four-square;
And uncomplaining, iron-shod,
Marched with Rome's honour for your god.

No bigot! In barbarian lands,
Roman where Rome no longer stands,
This altar to your hard-won love:
Earth, and the Nymphs and Springs thereof.

THE PHOENIX

WAKEFUL, I saw my window sashed
   With silver light before sunrise,
When, suddenly, the Phoenix flashed
   A rainbow streak across the skies;

81

And it was gone before I said:
   The Phoenix! In a book I read
The night before, I learnt to trace
That marvel to the happy place
It flies in, neither linde nor lawn
Of Earth, but in the Groves of Dawn.

There are so many things, the sight
   Goes clean through as it were X-ray:
The finer things that hide in light,
   Or in the heaven, that one might say,
Invisible, but we who know
How heedlessly the sight can go,
Employ the mind's eye but to find
That we are marvellously blind.

There are so many things that I
   Could see that now seem to be hid,
I feel that they would crowd the sky
   If I but lifted up a lid,
Or sang a song, or gave a shout,
That I would see them standing out;
But, as it is, what have I done
With all I've seen under the sun?

The Spring that comes before the Spring
   And waits while boughs are thin and bare,
A deepened light, a quickening,
   Annunciation in the air,
Delights me more, though cold and brief,
Than buds abounding, and the leaf.

And then the silver isles out far
   On leaden edge of Eastern seas,
Beneath a dappled sky, which are
   Our daily lost Atlantides,

The Phoenix

A moment seen, and they are gone,
Bright archipelagos of dawn,
Are more to me, and solider,
Than the near hills which never stir.

But would there be this seeking for,
    This wistful straining after things:
Islands surmised from lines of shore,
    Unless within me there were wings,
Wings that can fly in, and belong
Only to realms revealed by song,
That bring those realms about their nest,
Merging the Seeker and the Quest?

They beat in faintly purple air;
    Beneath them rise autumnal trees;
But Autumn's colours usher there
    A Spring which is Eternity's,

A Spring which overtakes the fruit,
Till blossoms crown the fond pursuit.
And there is neither Time nor Space
Within that paradisal place;
Nor separating length and breadth;
With Love identical is Death;
And no more fearful in that grove
Is Death to those who dwell than Love.

Not in our East then, but in verse,
    The far-seen flashing feather flies,
In Groves of Dawn whose wells immerse
    The star that lights and leads the Wise.
But rare's the book that holds the Word
That moves the uncompanioned Bird
To shake the air, and, in its flight,
Rain down the variegated light

That makes all timeless, and transforms
Unmagical and ageing norms;
And, when it falls upon, renews
The full blue eye, the twinkling thews,
And makes again the heart of man
Ageless and epinikian.

FRESH FIELDS

I GAZE and gaze when I behold
The meadows springing green and gold
I gaze until my mind is naught
But wonderful and wordless thought!
Till, suddenly, surpassing wit,
Spontaneous meadows spring in it;
And I am but a glass between
Un-walked-in meadows, gold and green.

HIGH TIDE AT MALAHIDE

(To Lynn Doyle)

THE luminous air is wet
As if the moon came through
To hold as in a net
Such as the spiders set
By ditch and rivulet,
The grey unfallen dew.
The sun is not down yet;
As yet the eve is new.

The water is all a-quiver,
There scarce is room to stand
Beside the tidal river
So narrowed is the strand:

84

And, over there, the wood
Is standing in a flood,
Erect, and upside down;
And at its roots, a swan.

A silvern mist enhances,
By tangling half the light,
The glowing bay's expanses
Which else had been too bright;
For air is subject to
A tidal ebb and flow.

And all the weeds with sandy root
That in the sunshine on the beach
Crackled like ashes underfoot,
Are standing upright now to stretch,
All ambered from within, each frond
That sways revived in the great pond;
And every axon in my brain
And neuron takes the tide again,
Made all the fuller from the tide
That brims the sands of Malahide;
But what shall come into it now
I know not. I await the flow.
I must abide the cosmic main
Whose high tide floods the stranded brain;
For no such miracle is wrought
On earth like this by taking thought.

Oh, look at the ships
With their sails coming down
And the wonderful sweeps
That are steering them still
To the little grey town
On the green of the hill!
Are they Norman or Norse,
Or descendants of Conn

Earth and Sea

Returning in force
From a lost British town,
With women and loot now the Roman is gone?
They are Norse! For the bugles are wild in the woods,
Alarms to the farms to look after their goods:
To bury their cauldrons and hide all their herds.
They are Norse! I can tell by the length of their swords—
Oh, no; by their spears and the shape of their shields
They are Normans: the men who stand stiff in the fields
In hedges of battle that no man may turn;
The men who build castles that no one may burn;
The men who give laws to the chief and the kern.
Salt of the earth,
Salt of the sea,
Norman and Norse
And the wild man in me!
The founders of cities,
The takers of fields,
The heroes too proud to wear armour or shields,
Their blood is in you,
As it cannot but be,
O Townsmen of towns on an estuary!

O clear Swords River that now without noise
Meets in this marvellous equipoise,
O clear Swords River, O let me know
What is it you add to the undertow,
For sight and sound like a bubble tost
On the high tide no more than on ether is lost:
No sight or odour or country sound
Lately reflected or long ago drowned,
But rises again, and as beautiful
As the golden weed when the tide is full,
Or the clouds that floating becalmed, sublime,
Break out white sails for the halcyon time.
With what do you mingle your merchandise

86

Of hawthorns budding or Autumn skies;
The cackling flight of the golden nib
That rallies the leaf to protect the crib;
The moth gone mad in a zigzag flight
On the magical edge of the day and the night;
The flag leaves serried beside your fords,
Like bronze gone green in the ancient swords;
The shadowless light of the peace to be;
The scent of the rain when it dries on the lea?
White wings are all that endow the sea,
Except when it grates on its soundless bars
Of diamonds shoaled from the fallen stars;
For all that you brought from the fields of home
Is saved, not lost, in the fields of foam,
And rises again, for it was not dead,
Here where the meadows and waters wed.
Remember that by no force terrene
Does the high tide rise till no sands are seen,
When silver limits the old green plain,
And the luminous mist floods into the brain
At will to replenish the Past again:
Such wonders cannot on earth be done
Till the moon join hands with the golden sun.

THE ISLES OF GREECE

Applied Poetry

(Lesbos)

MARBLE was her lovely city
And so pleasant was its air
That the Romans had no pity
For a Roman banished there;
Lesbos was a singing island
And a happy home from home

With the pines about its highland
And its crescent faint with foam.
Lady make a nota bene
That Love's lyric fount of glee
Rose in marbled Mytilene
Channelled by the purple sea.
Sappho sang to her hetairai,
And each lovely lyricist
Sappho's singing emulated;
And this point must not be missed:
Women were emancipated
Long before the Christian era,
Long before the time of Christ.
Then not only were they equal
To their men folk but themselves;
And the lovely lyric sequel
Lives on all our learned shelves.
Yes: we may be fairly certain,
As results of this release,
Sappho's was, with all its Girton
Girls, the fairest Isle of Greece.

II

Ah, those Isles of Asia Minor!
Was there ever such a coast?
Dawned there any day diviner
On a blither singing host?
Do not give this thought an inning
Lest the critics take it wrong:
In proportion to the sinning
Is the excellence of song.
Sin had not yet been imported
In those days to the Levant,
So the singers loved and sported,
Raised the paean, rhymed the chant,

Until Hebrew fortune tellers
Terrorised the pleasant scene,
Hawking horrors as best-sellers,
Mixing bards and baths with sin.
Therefore pass no moral stricture
On that fairest of Earth's states;
And succumb not to the mixture
Of ideas up with dates.

We shall find as we go boating
(You are paying for the yacht),
That those isles on purple floating
Were the isles of guiltless thought,
Isles whereby a peacock's feather
Would, if cast into the bay,
In the green and purple weather
Be reduced to hodden gray.
Gloomy thoughts are just a failing
From which you must win release
If with me you would come sailing
Carefree through the Isles of Greece.
Therefore pass no surly sentence
From our time and towns fog-pent,
Much less ask for their repentance
Who had nothing to repent.

THE WAVELESS BAY

(Kiltymon)

I close my eyes to hold a better sight,
And all my mind is opened on a scene
Of oaks with leaves of amber in the green,
A mist of blue beneath them: to the right

Earth and Sea

A long cape fades beyond the azurite
Of one calm bay to which the pastures lean.
The rounded fields are warm, and in between
The yellow gorse is glaring stiff and bright.
It matters little what distraction drives,
Clouds through my mind and breaks the outer day.
For all I know that distant water strives
Against the land.   I have it all my way:
Through budding oaks a steadfast sun survives:
Peace on the fading cape, the waveless bay.

FOG HORNS

THE fog horns sound
With a note so prolonged
That the whole air is thronged,
And the sound is to me,
In spite of its crying,
The most satisfying,
The bravest of all the brave sounds of the sea.

From the fjords of the North
The fogs belly forth
Like sails of the long ships
That trouble the earth.
They stand with loose sail
In the fords of the Gael:
From Dark Pool to White Ford the surf-light is pale.

The chronicles say
That the Danes in their day
Took a very great prey
Of women from Howth.
They seem to imply
That the women were shy,

That the women were loath
To be taken from Howth.
From bushy and thrushy, sequestering Howth.
No mists of the Druid
Could halt or undo it
When long ships besetted
The warm sands wave-netted.
In vain might men pray
To be spared the invader
To that kind eye of gray,
To the Saint who regretted
Sea-purple Ben Edar.
They sailed to the town
That is sprung from the sea
Where the Liffey comes down
Down to roll on the Lea.

The fog horns sound
With the very same roar
That was sounded of yore
When they sounded for war.
As the war horns sounded
When men leapt ashore,
And raised up the stane
Where the long ships had grounded.
You hear them again
As they called to the Dane,
And the glens were astounded.
War horns sounded,
And strong men abounded
When Dublin was founded.

Whenever a woman of Moore Street complains
With hawser of hair
Where the golds and browns are,
And under her arm

A sieve or a dish
Full of flowers or of fish,
I think of that ancient forgotten alarm:
Of horror and grief
As she snatched at the leaf
In tunnels sea-ended that fall to the reef.

It was all Long Ago,
Only now to the slow
Groping in of·the ships
In the sunlight's eclipse,
Are the fog horns sounded;
When war horns sounded
War ships could be grounded,
And dynasties founded.
But now they crawl in
With a far louder din
Than the old horns' could be;
And that's as it should be,
Because we put now
In the place of the prow
Of the dragon-head boats
A bowsprit of notes
With their loud, Safety First!
Where blue-eyed men burst,
And founded a city and founded a thirst!
And founded far more than to-day could be found:
The lesser the courage, the louder the sound!

But when the Dark Linn
Is aloud from the Rinn
I think of the women the sea-kings brought in:
The women of Dublin, the women who mother
A breed that the land and the sea cannot bother.
In flagons that ream
Like my own river's stream,

That gold of the granite
Gone black in the bogs,
I drink to our Race
That will go to the dogs,
Unless it can trace
And revive the old ways
Of the city when only
The bravest could man it,
Unless it can hold
To the virtues of old
When women resisted
And lovers were bold;
And steer through each upstart
Miasma that clogs
Its mind with the ravings
Of sly pedagogues;
And blow its own trumpet
To shatter the fogs.

BETWEEN BRIELLE AND MANASQUAN

THE old sea captains, when their work
    Was done on the eternal sea,
Came each ashore and built a house
    And settled down reluctantly;
And in his front lawn each set up
A flagstaff and a telescope.

Each little house was painted white
    With shutters gay and pointed gables
From which the vines hung loose or tight
    Or twisted round like coiled-up cables;
And each green lawn was so well drest
It seemed a little sea at rest.

And some were stocky men with beards
   And some were tawny, blue-eyed men;
And, when they talked, you might have heard
   Surnames that end in "-ing" or "-sen";
All sensed, since they had left the scene,
A falling off in things marine.

You cannot find their houses now
   The place is so much built upon,
They lived—they say who ought to know—
   Between Brielle and Manasquan;
But you can find, in some old store,
The curious things they brought ashore:

Old compasses, chronometers,
   And here a sextant ornamented,
A binnacle and carven wares,
   A captain's spy glass, rather dented,
A keg that raxed a pirate's throttle,
A schooner full rigged in a bottle:

Weapons with silver work inlaid;
   Blue glass the dealer says is Bristol's,
Carved shells and bits of Chinese jade;
   Two old, brass-barrelled, flint-lock pistols,
And, if these fail to take your fancy,
A figurehead called *Spumy Nancy*.

These old seafarers in their day,
   If asked about impressions wrought
By isles of Ind or far Cathay
   Could give no record of their thought;
What wonder worker ever knows
The wonder of the things he does?

94

Aye; but the little children knew
   What deep lagoons they anchored in,
What reefs they took their vessels through,
   And of strange cargoes hard to win;
The Isles of Spice, typhoons and thunder,
The Yellow Sea, and all its wonder.

They came to think, as they grew old
   And found themselves with few compeers,
That things grow better when they're told,
   And they themselves improved with years;
They'd sail again, did it beseem
Experienced men to take to steam.

Meanwhile, the long deserted sea
   Resented them as one neglected;
She swished her tides resentfully
   And tons and tons of sand collected
And silted up the narrow way
That leads to Barnagat's still Bay.

So that they lived as men marooned:
   They could not sail now if they hankered;
You'd think, to see their homes festooned,
   A fleet was in the Bay and anchored,
So gaily grew the creepers mounting,
So gaily flew the flagstaffs' bunting.

EARTH AND SEA

It lifts the heart to see the ships
   Back safely from the deep sea main;
To see the slender mizzen tips,
   And all the ropes that stood the strain;

To hear the old men shout "Ahoy,"
    Glad-hearted at the journey's end,
And fix the favourite to the buoy,
    Who had the wind and sea to friend;

To meet, when sails are lashed to spars,
    The men for whom Earth's free from care,
And Heaven a clock with certain stars,
    And Hell a word with which to swear.

THE SHIP

A SHIP from Valparaiso came
    And in the Bay her sails were furled;
She brought the wonder of her name,
    And tidings from a sunnier world.

O you must voyage far if you
    Would sail away from gloom and wet,
And see beneath the Andes blue
    Our white, umbrageous city set.

But I was young and would not go;
    For I believed when I was young
That somehow life in time would show
    All that was ever said or sung.

Over the golden pools of sleep
    She went long since with gilded spars;
Into the night-empurpled deep,
    And traced her legend on the stars.

But she will come for me once more,
    And I shall see that city set,
The mountainous, Pacific shore—
    By God, I half believe it yet!

OFF SICILY

SHELLS tilted up by Venus' heel
   Seen through the milk of morning air;
White Sicily confronts our keel
   With twin cliffs rising, each as fair
As that smooth-lined up-tilted boat
From which the Foam-Born Queen stept out.

But who can land where I am bound?
   In vain the natives tread their home.
They shall not find its holy ground,
   Who have not sought it in the tome
Whose letters twist like curls that deck
The nape of Venus' golden neck.

KINGDOMS

THE sailor tells the children
   His stories of the sea,
Their eyes look over the water
   To where his wonders be:

The flowers as big as tea-cups,
   The great big butterflies,
The long unfooted beaches
   Where stored-up treasure lies.

More than a thousand islands
   Each curved around its pool:
All kingdoms filled with sunlight,
   Where no one goes to school;

97

Earth and Sea

The fish that leave the water
In sudden bends of light
The birds as blue as china;
The flies that gleam by night . . .

Till, slowly, I remember
A wistful place; and then,—
The story of that Kingdom
First told to longshoremen.

SATIRES AND FACETIAE

O BOYS! O BOYS!

O BOYS, the times I've seen!
The things I've done and known!
If you knew where I have been?
Or half the joys I've had,
You never would leave me alone;
But pester me to tell,
Swearing to keep it dark,
What . . . but I know quite well:
Every solicitor's clerk
Would break out and go mad;
And all the dogs would bark!

There was a young fellow of old
Who spoke of a wonderful town,
Built on a lake of gold,
With many a barge and raft
Afloat in the cooling sun,
And lutes upon the lake
Played by such courtesans . . .
The sight was enough to take
The reason out of a man's
Brain; and to leave him daft,
Babbling of lutes and fans.

The tale was right enough:
Willows and orioles,
And ladies skilled in love:

But they listened only to smirk,
For he spoke to incredulous fools,
And, maybe, was sorry he spoke;
For no one believes in joys,
And Peace on Earth is a joke,
Which, anyhow, telling destroys;
So better go on with your work:
But Boys! O Boys ! O Boys!

RINGSEND

(After reading Tolstoi)

I WILL live in Ringsend
With a red-headed whore,
And the fan-light gone in
Where it lights the hall-door;
And listen each night
For her querulous shout,
As at last she streels in
And the pubs empty out.
To soothe that wild breast
With my old-fangled songs,
Till she feels it redressed
From inordinate wrongs,
Imagined, outrageous,
Preposterous wrongs,
Till peace at last comes,
Shall be all I will do,
Where the little lamp blooms
Like a rose in the stew;
And up the back-garden
The sound comes to me
Of the lapsing, unsoilable,
Whispering sea.

AFTER GALEN

ONLY the Lion and the Cock,
As Galen says, withstand Love's shock.
So, Dearest, do not think me rude
If I yield now to lassitude,
But sympathise with me. I know
You would not have me roar, or crow.

ON TROY

I GIVE more praise to Troy's redoubt
For Love kept in, than War kept out.

TO A BOON COMPANION

IF medals were ordained for drinks,
Or soft communings with a minx,
Or being at your ease belated,
By Heavens, you'd be decorated.
And not Alcmena's chesty son
Have room to put your ribbands on!

TO AN OLD TENOR

MELFORT DALTON, I knew you well
With your frozen eyes and your spastic stance.
Ah, but your voice was clear as a bell
When you tenored the ladies into a trance;
The finest tenor in town you were,
Finest; but those were the days of yore,

Oh, but weren't you arrogant then,
Weren't you arrogant, Chanticleer,
When you told each hostess to go to hell:
"I'll sing what I like and I'll read the score"?
Little they knew; but I knew what you meant:
Yourself you first had to magnify
Before your notes unto Heaven were sent—
(Peacocks and tenors and G.P.I.)
I knew it, and that is the reason why
I now am recording the wonderful tale
Of how you received an offer to come,
Though your eyes and your legs were beginning to
    fail,
And sing at St. Joseph's Old Maids' Home,
And all the honours you gained therefrom.

We sat in the nearest respectable bar
Waiting the message of how you fared;
And, though we wished it, we were not for
Success overwhelming quite prepared.
Sitting we waited and tippled the ale;
In came the scout with the wonderful word
Of how they tittered and how you scored:
"Called back four times." And we roared, "Waes-hael!
Melfort has done it again, good Lord!"
We were not allowed in the Old Maids' Home;
And rightly so, for they might be scared;
But "Here, boy, here. Tell us all How Come?"
"He shuffled at first, then he came to a stand.
He did not bow as a fav'rite should
(He knew that his balance was none too good)
But he stared with a visage inane and bland."
"But how did he merit such great applause?
Be more explicit, you poor recorder?"
"Once for singing, and thrice because
His dress revealed a quaint disorder."

To an Old Tenor

Moral

(*Non Nobis*)

A moral lies in this occurrence:
Let those who have too much assurance
And think that public approbation
That comes from songs or an oration
Is due but to their own desert,
Remember Melfort Dalton's shirt.

TO A MUSHROOM

No one sang thee, little fielding,
  Sang thy wondrous being and birth,
Till to mute attraction yielding
  I first hymned thee here on earth.

Though I never saw thee start up,
  I have seen thee when thou wert
Poised as with an hinder part up—
  Oh my sudden quaint upstart!

In the short grass by the fount-head
  Thou art found as free from rule
As a faun, and unaccounted
  As a little boy from school.

Or a baby plump and ample,
  Whose exuberance was led
By Silenus' bad example
  Till the bowl fell o'er his head

Of all growing things the oddest;
  Only of a sudden seen
Unexpected and immodest
  As above a stocking, skin!

Soft, I must entreat thee gently;
  For I can but do thee wrong,
And but think inconsequently
  Who for daylight pitch my song.

Suns for thee must still illume an
  Arid waste beneath the sky,
Wistful, cold and thwartly human
  And Augustan—even as I.

Darkness only does not flout thee
  When alone thou tak'st the light,
And the silence floats about thee,
  Moon-loved dewy child of night.

Thine example shows quite clearly,
  That the things we think deranged
Would be most delightful merely,
  Merely if the scene were changed.

TO THE MAIDS NOT TO WALK IN THE WIND

When the wind blows, walk not abroad,
For, Maids, you may not know
The mad, quaint thoughts which incommode
Me when the winds do blow.

What though the tresses of the treen
In doubled beauty move,
With silver added to their green,
They were not made for Love.

But when your clothes reveal your thighs
And surge around your knees,
Until from foam you seem to rise,
As Venus from the seas . . .

Though ye are fair, it is not fair!
Unless you will be kind,
Till I am dead, and changed to AIR,
O walk not in the wind!

THE NETTLE

A VERY pleasant hillside falls among
Pines to the south, and in a greensward settles;
And while we loitered there my Love was stung,
My girl-Adonis on the thigh by nettles.
O what a bore! I must sit down, said she;
I cannot walk! . . . O darling, what's the matter?
A nettle stung me where you must not see,
Just where my stocking ends and thigh grows fatter.
But I will shut my eyes before it gets . . .
And you shall guide me so I shall not miss it—
Before the poison in your system sets,
I'll press my lips and very gently kiss it.
The little blister white upon the white
Of sudden snow where violets were peeping,
Was reddened by the cure which set it right.
Now if, years hence, you find they are not keeping
My grave with all the reverence that is due
To one whom Beauty's smile in Life elated,
O, Busybody, trouble not! Can you
Be sure the nettle waves to desecrate it?

A PITHY PRAYER AGAINST LOVE

GODS, get me out of it!
Spirits of Laughter
Come to my aid now
And exorcise it!
O you, Priapus,
Stand till you're skyward,
Stand till you're all staff
And cannot rise it!
Let your preposterous
Pole fall upon her:
"That for her honour!"
Let not a thought now
Of comfort escape us:
Think what in boisterous,
Blowing Jack Falstaff,
Shakespeare made Love look.
Think how that cheerful
Chiel Hippocleides
Would this my fearful
Passion disparage;
Dancing incessantly,
Dancing indecently,
Danced, till he danced off
A cure for all heart-aches
(Dancing the cordax!),
Danced, till his carriage
Displeased the bride's father;
Dancing it further,
He danced off his marriage;
Danced to surmout his
Fate with: οὐ φροντίς!
Teach me his courage.

NEW FORMS

I GATHERED marble Venus in my arms,
Just as the rabble crowded on the stair.
I said, For her the sea gave up its storms;
And gently on her body breathed the air.
Alas, she fell, and broke to many pieces:
Discovered later by a Professor,
He cried, "New forms, new forms!" And wrote a thesis.

THE THREE

FAITH

BRIAN O'LYNN as the legends aver
Was crossing a bridge with his wife and his cur.
The bridge it collapsed and the trio fell in:
"There's land at the bottom," said Brian O'Lynn.

HOPE

Let Surgeon MacCardle confirm you in Hope.
A jockey fell off and his neck it was broke.
He lifted him up like a fine, honest man;
And he said "He is dead; but I'll do all I can."

CHARITY

Life would be less outrageous
If all the drinks were free;
And Health became contagious
And Old Age fit to see;
And, when we stretched our tether,
Instead of loitering,
All we went all together
Like blossoms in the Spring.

CHORIC SONG OF THE LADIES OF LEMNOS

(The Lemnians having killed their husbands, faced with the necessity of defending the Island, resolve to press the crew of the Argo *which carried Hercules into marriage.)*

STR. I.   WHO will marry Hercules?
    Tell me if you can.
Who will catch his eye, and please
    The strong silent man?

Who will make a happy home,
    For duty and desire:
In Summer tend the honey-comb,
    In Winter, tend the fire?

ANTIS. I.   What exactly is the sense,
    And substance of your song?
Is his strength in reticence;
    Or is he silent, strong?

Often strong and silent men,
    With sorra much to say,
Are with young and old women
    Winsome in their way.

EPOS. I.   'Tis the great Tirynthian groom,
    A boyo hard to parry!
Rather ask the question whom
    Hercules will marry.

STR. II.   Thus to speak as if no choice
    Were left, is to disparage

Choric Song of the Ladies of Lemnos

Us, who surely have a voice,
  And the half of marriage;

To put the cart before the horse,
  The groom before the bride.
It is for the girl, of course,
  Also to decide.

ANTIS. II. O look at him with his club,
      And his lion's fell!
    That's the lad who made the hub-
      Bub below in Hell!

    That which is the pirates' quest
      May be Hercules's:
    To carry off the buxomest,
      And marry whom he pleases!

EPOS. II. Praise him for his shoulders' breadth,
    Him who took the Town of Death,
    Took the triple Dog therefrom,
    And Alcestis to her home.

    Praise him, for he carries through
    All he sets himself to do;
    No one ever saw him chuck
    Anything he undertook;

    Softly talk of marriage, he
    Might embrace the colony;
    And if he were duly roused
    Who would then be unespoused?

111

EUROPA AND THE BULL

(To Arthur Train)

"WHERE is little Wide Eyes?"
"Where but in the farmyard."
"Have I never told you
To be careful of the child?"
"Well, you would not think that
There she would come harmward,
If you saw the stallion tremble
When she pats him, and grow mild."

"Nurse, it's not of danger
From animals I'm thinking;
Rather of a fashion
Which of late has grown too rife:
Girls of county families,
Of men in my position,
With grooms are so familiar,
It's as bad as man and wife!

And then there is this Never-to-be-
Too-much-deprecated
Tendency towards bringing
Only daughters up as boys;
If the Queen were living,
She would never tolerate it. . . .
What's their masquerading
To the magic it destroys!"

"Well I know that queer things
Happen in the country:
Nothing could be queerer
Than a King to take his cue
From his subjects' families,
Or pardon their effrontery

Who dared to tell his daughter
Or her Nannie what to do."

"I, not unobservant,
Nurse, have noticed anger
Often used by women
Who were not irascible,
Out of mere resentment
When they could no longer
Argue a position
Which had proved untenable.

If your speech is ended,
Listen, my good woman,
Nothing is achieved by
Incoherent talk:
Tell her that the country
Is an open farmyard,
Wide Eyes will go with you
And her maidens for a walk.

Any distance inland
Needs the stoutest buskin,
Sandals are more suited
To the firmly-sanded shore;
No matter where you go to,
Surely come by dusk in.
I trust we need not talk about
The farmyard any more."

     *   *   *

Dunes are here on this side,
There, that piny headland;
Midway, like a giant,
Is that landward-leaning tree,
Angry with the constant
Briny-blowing West Wind,
Poising up a shoulderstone
To cast it in the sea.

Do you see that wave there,
Where the crescent curves lift,
Transilluminating
For a second into green
Miles of crystal daylight,
Then, the hissing snowdrift:
Light so water-tangled
That its sightless self is seen—?

That is how the daylight,
Barely vespertinal,
Save but for a feeling
That a moon was very near,
Looked above the headland
Of the sandy, sinal
Crescent, while it waited
For a crescent in the air.

Taller than the tallest
Of her young companions,
Wide Eyes never wilted
Where the broken ground begins:
That's the Archer Goddess,
With her bosom belted!
No; it is a tomboy
With the scratches on her shins!

Certainly unconscious
That she was a maiden
Who could fill with banners
Frontiers of Kings!
Once you saw ner swinging
From her youthful haunches,
You would feel that manners
Were not all-important things.

Europa and the Bull

"If I raced you up there,
Which of you could whistle?
Just you watch me running
When I get my second wind."
Moulding in her short skirt
Limbs to jump the thistle,
A cry of wonder reached her
From the little group behind.

Gambolling and charging,
Low head shaken sideways,
Swerving as though guided
By his tassel rudder tail,
Snorting more than stamping
A ripple on the tideways,
A Bull, where nothing ever
Drew a furrow but a sail!

Eyes beneath a broad brow
Widen with amazement,
Not because the women
Who were with her ran away;
But because a bull used
Water for a pavement.
Down the fearless maiden went
To meet him at the Bay.

White as any Maytree
In the milky Maytime,
Clothed about her middle
With a dress as deep as haws,
On the beach she waited
In the silver of the daytime,
A blurred green moon above her
Like a May branch in the shaws.

Clear against the bright wall
Of the low horizon
On the bull came, prancing,
Lifting up his knees.
He came on as gaily
As a galley dancing
While its sail is being lowered
And the shouts are from the quays.

Like a man of Yorkshire
Grunting after Christmas,
When the curly foreheads
And the appetites convene,
White against the dark green
Pines along the isthmus;
He landed hardly wetted
By his gambols on the brine.

Beating Heart of Nature
What is it divorced us
From your mighty pulses
Throbbing into Sense!
Sorra much the Hermit,
Reason gives, who cursed us:
Even Love goes ebbing
From his deadly prescience!

Now he runs around her,
Now he stands before her,
Now his mighty breathings
Tighten up her clothes;
Now he runs around her,
Now he kneels before her,
Now she pulls her instep
From the spraying of his nose!

Europa and the Bull

Who except a fool would
Think he knew the mental
Processes that act upon
A widow, wife or maid?
But the very sight of
Strength becoming gentle—
That is what they can't resist:
A married man has said.

Not the alabaster
Palaces of Minos
Ever held a better
Or a bull more quickly tamed:
Glancing coat half-ruffled
Like a pool amid the spinous
Dells of Ida's island
For a hundred cities famed.

From his dewlap only
Drops of water trickled,
For she felt his back warm,
Silky-soft and dry,
And no common bull's hide!
For it never tickled,
When she held the strong beast
Tight with either thigh.

Maybe, had she noticed,
When she first went near him,
That he had no halter
Nor the ring he should have worn,
She might have cast about her
For another way to steer him:
Bulls are ill-directed
When you take them by the horn.

Once he had her mounted,
Even had she willed it,
She could not have left him
While the sea was yet below,
But she held on lightly
To the garlands on the gilded
Horns, more blunt, but stronger
Than the horns of buffalo.

Some wondered was she laughing at
The bucketing and heaving
Bull who tried her courage
When he sent the waves aswirl;
Some wondered was she sorry for
The home that she was leaving:
All talk! They only wondered
What would happen to the girl!

Because the tales that suit me best
Are tales without a moral.
Like this—unless at Harmony
It hints in times afar,
Before with all creation
And ourselves we came to quarrel;
Before the animals found out
What animals we are.

Because I love the days in which
Such miracles were common,
Because I can suggest to you,
So sceptical of all,
(The mind provides the prodigy)
That many a horsey woman
Would welcome well such miracle
When riding for a fall—;

Because the thoughts I dwell upon
Would never pass a teacher
Who maintains the World was made
According to the word
Of men who separate Mankind
From Universal Nature—
For what eloping god to-day
Would turn into a Ford?

Because I hold an Age of Faith
Whose dogma is emphatic
Is happier than such as this
When, if there's faith about,
'Tis not in gods by girls transformed,
But Jewish mathematic,
I go for Truth to Beauty
Which is subject to less doubt.

So I see the white Bull
As the water yellowed
With the purple-vested
Girl upon his back,
Laughing when he dipt down,
Laughing when he bellowed,
Laughing when she dug her heels
To goad him on the track.

Peace instead of panic now
Where, long ago, erumpent
Through the trance of quiet
Of that farmstead with a roar—
Sand instead of cities since—
The Bull bore off triumphant
That sweet and self-made burden
From the blest Sidonian shore.

What about her father?
Formal proclamation
That it was her nurse's
Fault was no excuse
In the eyes of "County,"
Nor a consolation;
But glory when the Church declared
His son-in-law was Zeus!

THE OLD WOMAN OF BEARE

(From the Irish)

(*This to-day had been Fresh Nellie,*
For she had as wild a belly;
Or a kind of Mrs. Mack,
For she had a bonnie back;
Or the Honourable Mrs. Lepple—
Nipple to a kingly nipple—
For she never took advantage
Of the favours of her frontage;
Therefore she was held in honour
By the warty boys who won her;
Therefore some old Abbey's shelf
Kept the record of herself,
Telling to men who disapprove
Of Love, the long regrets of Love.)

Now my tide of youth is gone
And my ebb of age comes on;
Though the sonsie may be happy,
I'm no longer soft and sappy.

The Old Woman of Beare

Age is causing all my woes:
I who had new underclothes
As I queened it every day,
Now have no one's castaway.

O the times that I had then!
You have money, I had men
Who could give their horse the reins
Yet not leave their own demesnes.

Of the men for whom I stript
None was weaker when we clipt,
But the fury of my flame
Magnified the man in him.

Now each bargain-driving clown
Wants two ups for one go down;
God, if I reciprocated,
They would think themselves castrated!

All my thoughts are of the years
When we drove the brazen cars:
Of the gold we used to fling;—
What was money to a king?

Now my arms are flat and dried
Which were round on every side,
Dearer once to kings than gems,
Dearer than their diadems.

Shameful now to lift them up
Round the hairless neck of youth;
Though my name may be a lure,
I am no boy's paramour.

See the careless lassies swing
As they walk the lane of Spring;
See the lassies go a-Maying
Safe awhile from Time's waylaying!

Once I never heard of stints
On my colours or my pints.
Particolours I could wear;
Now what colour is my hair?

I've no grudge against old age;
But what puts me in a rage
Is that women flaunt their gold
Heads before me when I'm old.

Kings are under Femen's stone;
Bregon holds their weathered throne;
The very stones are worse for wear,
And dappled grey is Bregan's Chair.

A wave stands up and shouts at sea:
It's Winter here for more than me!
I have no sheets; but, as I say,
McHugh will hardly call to-day.

The lads I loved are all aboard,
And strain through Alma's reedy ford;
No logs of oak will break and glow
To warm the beds where they are now!

There's not one left of all the band
That well could bring a boat to strand
Where I ran with little on
Who now am cloaked even in the sun.

Now whatever comes to me
Must be met with "Glory be!"
Glory be to God at least
For each feat of old, and feast.

Glory be! I'm half content
Just to think of all I spent.
Passion never waned in me
For the want of . . . Glory be!

Every foot that moves must stop;
Every acorn has to drop;
For the blazing festive sconce
Darkness now, and prayer's response.

Cups of whey at night and morn
For the crescent drinking horn;
But the nuns and all their whey
Have not washed my rage away!

YOUTH AND TRUTH

WHEN I was young the trees would bend
And shake their branches merrily;
As if they knew I was their friend
They stretched their little hands to me;
Grasses would run across the brake,
And little waves dance on the lake.
Then someone said, "It is the wind."
Oh, why should Truth be so unkind?

JOB'S HEALER

WHEN the Comforters of Job
Had filled up each weary lobe
With suggestions, there appeared—
Goatee foot and goatee beard—
Most appropriately from mist,
Satan, the Psychiatrist.

He said, "I've seen and overheard
How you look, and every word
You have uttered makes me guess
I can help you in distress.
First, let not your mind be bumptious:
Jonah, gulphed by his Subconscious,
Stands for fact.   The parable
Is, of course, the whopping Whale.
Your Subconscious is your trouble
Which your Reason can but double.
Let us now proceed to state it;
Then we'll try to sublimate it.

Oh, your instinct was so right
When you cursed conception night,
For the source of all your bother
Is, of course, your lady Mother.
She craved, just before her wedding,
Highballs and a whole plum pudding;
And that ante-natal wish
Lands you in this kettle o' fish.
For, you know, too many Scotches
Make the skin come out in blotches:
Confluent furunculosis
Is the rest of your psychosis,
Which may represent the plums
In that pudding of your Mum's.

Job's Healer

Things that on the land and sea go
Are projections of your Ego:
Leviathan and Behemoth—
You may add the Lord to both—
And we get three combinations
Of immense hallucinations.
God is merely a convention
That produces inward tension,
Or a goal man cannot match
Just to keep him up to scratch;
Else, he might be just as thievish
As you're itchy, old and peevish.

Sing this little song with me,
'Since there is no diety
What's the use of piety?
Or of goodness, or of badness?
Either way can lead to madness
As Responsibility
Leads to imbecility.
Long ago against Free Will
Mankind took a sleeping pill.
It is time he took another
Sleeping pill against his Mother.

Every man from woman came,
Only woman is to blame.
Every thing's hereditary
Therefore, eat, drink and be merry.'

Since your mind can now perceive
Only evil comes from Eve,
Borrow an ax,
With a couple of whacks
Kill your mother
And then,
RELAX!"

LOVE AND BEAUTY

Love and Beauty

DEDICATION

TALL unpopular men,
Slim proud women who move
As women walked in the islands when
Temples were built to Love,
I sing to you.   With you
Beauty at best can live,
Beauty that dwells with the rare and few,
Cold and imperative.
He who had Cæsar's ear
Sang to the lonely and strong.
Virgil made an austere
Venus Muse of his song.

THINKING LONG

WHEN children call you, Grandmamma;
And you with thin dark-veinèd hands
In silence stroke the heads that, Ah!
Recall the glorious smouldering bands
Of sullen gold that bound your brow,
And him who told you how the light
Burst through them when you combed them low
With sidelong head at fall of night:
Before that vision fades away

129

Just take this message from the Past:
"'Tis love that counteracts decay
And lights and makes all Beauty last."
And wonder if the love you spared
To starve the light-heart man of rhyme
Has left him low and you grey-haired,
Though you are old, before your time.

TELL ME NOW

SHE

TELL me now is Love's day done?
Beauty as elect and rare
As when towns were trampled on
Lives to-day and takes the air.
Yet no amorous Triumvir
Throws the world and Rome away;
No one swims Abydos' bay;
Towns are not cast down, and none,
None begets the Moon and Sun.

HE

Do not let him hear your taunt!
Love's as strong to-day as when
Walls could not endure his brunt,
And he broke the Trojan men.
He can do as much again;
Do not doubt him for an hour,
Tempt his pleasure, not his power;
Danger gives him no affront,
He is not cooled by Hellespont.

CONCERNING HERMIONE

I. THE CONQUEST

"SINCE the Conquest none of us
Has died young except in battle."
I knew that hers was no mean house,
And that beneath her innocent prattle
There was likely hid in words
What could never anger Fame;
The glory of continuous swords,
The obligations of a name.
Had I grown incredulous,
Thinking for a little space:
Though she has the daring brows,
She has not the falcon face;
In the storm from days of old
It is hard to keep at poise,
And it is the over-bold,
Gallant-hearted, Fate destroys:
Could I doubt that her forbears
Kept their foot-hold on the sands,
Triumphed through eight hundred years,
From the hucksters kept their lands,
And still kept the conquering knack—
I who had myself gone down
Without waiting the attack
Of their youngest daughter's frown?

II. EXORCISM

To banish your shape from my mind
  I thought of the dangerous wood
Where a man might wander and find,
  By a stream in the solitude,

131

The Queen it is death if one sees,
    Death by a merciless dart;
But how could that bring me release,
    Shot as I am to the heart?

Beauty will cure me, I cried;
    By Beauty is Beauty dislodged.
And I worked on a dream till I eyed
    The Queens whom the young man judged.
But the vision faded and slipt;
    And the cure was a cure of no worth;
For I said, when the Queens were stript,
    I have given the prize to a fourth.

Ugliness, Chaos and War
    I know, but I would not invoke;
They would feed you as darkness a star,
    And strengthen the beam of my yoke.
If Love be reborn in a song
    I with my fate will not quarrel,
But you, if you do him a wrong,
    May be changed to a reed or a laurel.

III. EXCOMMUNICATION

Go to the fields of purple and gold;
    With lovers and young Queens remain,
Blossoms and battlements of old,
    Far in the background of my brain.
Rest with them there, but stand apart,
    Although you equal those who died;
For no one enters in my heart
    By Death or Love undeified.

IV. SILENCE

The purple falls between the pines,
The sun that blanched Arundel walls,

132

Remembering them as he declines,
With purple fills his airy halls.
We drove all day; and all day long
Of Love and longing long we spoke;
And sang so often ballad and song,
The crescent moon cannot evoke
Another word; though Beauty calls
There is no word that can be said.
If Hesperus unhailed shines on,
O do not dream that Love is dead.
The hand I take is not withdrawn,
Between the pines the purple falls.

V. A SOUND

She called me by my Christian name,
    Quite simply of her own accord,
And unexpectedly it came—
    O the exceeding great reward!
Where are the years of longing, years
    Of vigils and anxieties,
My perturbations now, my fears?
    Gone with the wind across the trees.
Enchanted now, I walk in peace,
    As one who walking on a sward
At twilight hears, or thinks he hears,
    A fanfare out of Joyous Gard.

RELEASE

(To Calypso)

NOT fixed is worship as I thought
When first your pride I faced,
But by some wonder heaven-wrought
May be at once displaced.

133

The heart to one ideal tied
May be released one day;
One day the Messenger, espied
Above Pieria,

Shall stoop; and, as he skims and dips—
Each sandal's golden fin
Fanning the violet water tips
To rainbows as they spin—

Come with the order from above;
And, like Odysseus, free,
I for an human-hearted love
Again shall risk the sea!

MELSUNGEN

Love, let us go to the village of Melsungen,
Folded in the river which is flowing without noise:
Dark are the woods and the fields are green and golden,
Spreading to the ripple of the hills against the skies.

Hold down the car on the long road to Melsungen;
Hold the heart down that no speed can ever sate!
Through the noon already it has raced into the evening,
Raced, and reached the gables in the evening falling late.

Long have I gazed at your window in Melsungen,
Yellow in the lamp-light, while I watch the miles at noon,
Dreaming of peace as the arrow from the bow-string
Dreams, and gains in quiet from the speed which makes it
    swoon.

Love, let us lean from a dormer in Melsungen,
Giving on the valley where the light has found the stream,
Cool and becalmed, as the moonlight on the water,
Motionless and quiet as beyond our life a dream.

LEAVE TAKING

I PUSHED the leaves aside:
Upon a mountain lawn
I saw a little fawn
White-throated, vivid, pied.
"Her eyes are just as tender,
Her ankles just as slender,"
I said.   With challenged grace,
It fled before my face,
Slim-ankled, velvet-eyed.

I watched a topmost spray
Of leaves that move and shimmer
In faintest airs of Summer
Before the trance of day.
I said, "A curl can float
Breathless across her throat."
The silver leaves stopt glistening
As if they had been listening
To what I had to say.

A bank of tangled briars
Sloped gently to the south,
Its leaves recalled her mouth
With their soft hidden fires.
"Her lips are bright as cherries
And sweet as wild strawberries,"

I said. Where leaves were spangled
The wild rose grew more tangled
With barbed and bending wires.

From some rush-hidden spring
A stream in little trebles
Tinkled from pools of pebbles
And gurgled, preluding
Each laughing, liquid note,
Coiled in a woman's throat.
I said, "I hear her laughter";
And then, a moment after,
The stream began to sing.

The bank I rested on
Was gently curved and warm,
I dreamt about her form.
I said, "She has withdrawn
Into herself delight
And joy from every sight."
The wind that dusks the grasses
Tells when a spirit passes—
I felt that she was gone.

SEND FROM THE SOUTH . . .

SEND from the South warm thoughts to me
From alleys closed by Summer sea
Whence the great Gulf its Stream puts forth
Laden with Summers for the North;
And for the sun a purple throne
From which he may with joy look down,
Bending beyond his cloudy towers,
On main and islands fringed with flowers.

Send from the South warm thoughts to melt
The frost that all the more is felt
The farther off from you am I;
So that I may for solace sing
And to my heart your Summer bring;
For those whom distance parts too long
The only medicine is Song.

BEGONE, SWEET GHOST

BEGONE, sweet Ghost, O get you gone!
Or haunt me with your body on;
And in that lovely terror stay
To haunt me happy night and day.
For when you come I miss it most,
Begone, sweet Ghost!

But do not clothe you in the dress
Whereby was young Actaeon killed;
He died because of loveliness,
And I will die from that withheld,
Unless you take on flesh, unless
In that you dress!

GAZE ON ME

GAZE on me, though you gaze in scorn;
O Lady, fix on me those eyes,
And then the darkness may be borne
When two such glorious lights arise;
For is there one, if stars shine bright,
Who will not praise the dark of night?

As gloaming brings the bending dew,
That flowers may faint not in the sun,
So, Lady, now your looks renew
My heart, although it droops adown;
And thus it may unwithered be,
When you shall deign to smile on me.

BACK FROM THE COUNTRY

BACK from the country
Ruddy as an apple,
Looking ripe and rural
As the maid a farmer seeks;
Fresh as an apple
Shining in the pantry,
Back you came to Dublin
Whom I had not seen for weeks:
How I hid my laughter
Fearing to offend you,
Back from the country
With your apple cheeks!

GOOD LUCK

APPLES of gold the Hero dropt
    As he was in the race outstript;
And Atalanta, running, stopt,
    And all her lovely body dipt
A moment; but she lost her stride—
And had to go to bed a bride.

And was it not a cordial strong,
    By which the young Iseult was filled
With passion for a whole life long;
    For that the amorous juice instilled?
So he who kept the unwitting tryst
Was sure of love before he kissed.

But where can I get Western gold,
    Or posset of constraining fire?—
I who am fated to behold
    Beauty outdistancing desire?
Aye, and to falter wonder-struck;
There's no good love without good luck!

APPLIED POETRY

ALL thoughts of you are joys
    And wistful fun!
My heart is like a boy's,
    What have you done?

For I can no more think
    Of pounds and pence
Just now, than I can think
    With commonsense.

The leaves of forest glades
    Where you are seen
Are still light yellow blades
    Before their green;

Love and Beauty

Each soaking meadow pool
　　That's blurred with blue
To me, who am a fool,
　　The eyes of you!

The glistening breezes spilt
　　Through aspen tops
Where April kicks her quilt
　　Of buttercups

And makes the meadow sway
　　Its counterpane,—
As if Doll Tearsheet lay
　　And leapt again,

Are surely hints enough
　　That sweet and sure
Was he with: "Youth's a stuff
　　Will not endure."

So let us find a bank. . . .
　　What's this?　You won't?
You think I mean to rank—
　　Indeed I don't—

Doll Tearsheet with yourself,
　　My Dear, you're dull!
How could a lanky elf
　　Suggest a trull?

But she was meant to show,
　　(If Will gave lessons)
That only women know
　　The human essence,

And see beneath a part,
  Though clothed upon
By Evil, the rich heart
  Of gross Sir John;

Which no one else perceived.
  When he was sickly,
Who was it for him grieved
  But Doll and Quickly?

Significant and sad!
  But each descendant
Of Adam, good or bad,
  Is Eve's dependant.

We are a sorry race
  Whose horoscope,
Uncast by Woman's grace,
  Portends faint hope.

And now I find that he
  Who stole and cheated,
Compared with honest me
  Was kindlier treated. . . .

You used to love the Bard,
  Then more's the pity
That now you disregard
  What's blithe and witty!

And play the Grandmamma,
  Aloof, sedate:
"Our pleasant Willie, ah!
  Is dead in you of late!"

Love and Beauty

There! there! I don't suggest
    You are not fit to live
Up to the very best
    That life in Art can give.

See, there's a bank that's fenced,
    Wherein, whereon
Joy may be lodged against
    Oblivion;

And we hereafter, say
    That we of yore,
One slanting sunny day
    Could do no more

Than make this gentle bank
    Joy's strong redoubt
Which years may not outflank,
    Nor Memory flout.

" Well, to accomplish that
    What must we do?"
" We must do something pat,
    Something Come-to."

Love can't be made by proxy,
    Lest faith in Love should fail.
Heigh with the orthodoxy,
    Come with me o'er the dale!

The only way to capture
    What may not be expressed
Is turn it into rapture
    Or turn it into jest.

So when you're old and fading,
   A Christian Scientist,
Intent on self-persuading
   That Evil can't exist

And I, for all my slimming,
   Of somewhat stouter build,—
"To Rescue Fallen Women"—
   Am Chairman of—The Guild. . . .

(My Dear, we can't eschew it,
   For Fate is farcical.
The mighty poet knew it:
   There's Falstaff in us all.)

When, after much persuasion,
   In public we appear
To grace a State occasion,
   Both you and I, my Dear,

Well honoured and respected,
   We meet our troops of friends:
Since on the Undetected,
   Respect so much depends,

I'll give you formal greeting
   And bow while whispering
This spell: "My pretty sweeting!"
   To plunge our hearts in Spring;

For they, who hold together
   Half shares in Love's secret,
Can conjure Spring, and tether
   The years that bring regret.

TO SHADU 'L-MULK

(*Delight of the Kingdom*)
from the Persian of Khalil Shah

MY Loved One has another
    And a nameless paramour
Which causes me no bother,
    For she loves me all the more.

Thus, for the dam's rebellion,
    The ostlers often try her
With a jackass, till the stallion
    Strikes the cobbles into fire.

LEDA AND THE SWAN

THOUGH her Mother told her
    Not to go a-bathing,
Leda loved the river
    And she could not keep away:
Wading in its freshets
    When the noon was heavy;
Walking by the water
    At the close of day.

Where between its waterfalls,
    Underneath the beeches,
Gently flows a broader
    Hardly moving stream,
And the balanced trout lie
    In the quiet reaches;
Taking all her clothes off,
    Leda went to swim.

Leda and the Swan

There was not a flag-leaf
 By the river's margin
That might be a shelter
 From a passer-by;
And a sudden whiteness
 In the quiet darkness,
Let alone the splashing,
 Was enough to catch an eye.

But the place was lonely,
 And her clothes were hidden;
Even cattle walking
 In the ford had gone away;
Every single farm-hand
 Sleeping after dinner,—
What's the use of talking?
 There was no one in the way.

In, without a stitch on,
 Peaty water yielded,
Till her head was lifted
 With its ropes of hair;
It was more surprising
 Than a lily gilded,
Just to see how golden
 Was her body there:

Lolling in the water,
 Lazily uplifting
Limbs that on the surface
 Whitened into snow;
Leaning on the water,
 Indolently drifting,
Hardly any faster
 Than the foamy bubbles go.

Love and Beauty

You would say to see her
   Swimming in the lonely
Pool, or after, dryer,
   Putting on her clothes:
"O but she is lovely,
   Not a soul to see her,
And how lovely only
   Leda's Mother knows!"

Under moving branches
   Leisurely she dresses,
And the leafy sunlight
   Made you wonder were
All its woven shadows
   But her golden tresses,
Or a smock of sunlight
   For her body bare.

When on earth great beauty
   Goes exempt from danger,
It will be endangered
   From a source on high;
When unearthly stillness
   Falls on leaves, the ranger,
In his wood-lore anxious,
   Gazes at the sky.

While her hair was drying,
   Came a gentle languor,
Whether from the bathing
   Or the breeze she didn't know.
Anyway she lay there,
   And her Mother's anger
(Worse if she had wet hair)
   Could not make her dress and go.

Leda and the Swan

Whitest of all earthly
    Things, the white that's rarest,
Is the snow on mountains
    Standing in the sun;
Next the clouds above them,
    Then the down is fairest
On the breast and pinions
    Of a proudly sailing swan.

And she saw him sailing
    On the pool where lately
She had stretched unnoticed,
    As she thought, and swum;
And she never wondered
    Why, erect and stately,
Where no river weed was
    Such a bird had come.

What was it she called him:
    Goosey-goosey gander?
For she knew no better
    Way to call a swan;
And the bird responding
    Seemed to understand her,
For he left his sailing
    For the bank to waddle on.

Apple blossoms under
    Hills of Lacedaemon,
With the snow beyond them
    In the still blue air,
To the swan who hid them
    With his wings asunder,
Than the breasts of Leda,
    Were not lovelier!

Love and Beauty

Of the tales that daughters
  Tell their poor old mothers,
Which by all accounts are
  Often very odd;
Leda's was a story
  Stranger than all others.
What was there to say but:
  Glory be to God?

And she half-believed her,
  For she knew her daughter;
And she saw the swan-down
  Tangled in her hair.
Though she knew how deeply
  Runs the stillest water,
How could she protect her
  From the wingèd air?

Why is it effects are
  Greater than their causes?
Why should causes often
  Differ from effects?
Why should what is lovely
  Fill the world with harness?
And the most deceived be
  She who least suspects?

When the hyacinthine
  Eggs were in the basket,
Blue as at the whiteness
  Where a cloud begins;
Who would dream there lay there
  All that Trojan brightness;
Agamemnon murdered;
  And the mighty Twins?

FAITHFUL EVEN UNTO FREUD

EVEN judged by dreams which are
But phantasmal parodies
Of my life; and hollower
Than the glory of the skies
Which the seven maids maintain,
Heavenly sisters of the rain,

I am true. If you came in
To the Liberties of Sleep
Where, as proud as Saladin,
A preposterous state I keep;
Would you ever guess each bride
Was your own self multiplied?

Where, by water-lilies stilled,
Some forgotten old canal
Mirrors deep a window-silled
Maiden in a castle wall,
You again: but no disguise
Warms your willow-greenish eyes.

To a place where engineers
Coax a stream to climb a hill
And a marble reappears
Mountain-melted snowy still
Water, as before the Moor
Laid it on his rose-leaf floor,

I am banished beyond time,
To my faith an infidel;
Ruling in another clime
Devotees who serve me well,
Moving as they seek my love
Hips that like twin melons move.

With my boat's three-cornered sail
Shaped as is a rose's thorn,
While the morning yet is pale,
Gently filling, I am borne,
Where . . . it is not every man's
Luck to meet Corinthians.

Aphrodite's house is there;
She knows what you drove me to.
The most pleasant form of prayer
That a worshipper can do
Was enjoined. But nothing cures
Love the loved one still abjures.

FAREWELL TO THE PRINCESS

I WHO had your love,
Have now my pride;
And that is worthy of
All love denied.
Times change; but long ago
Men stood no suffering
That came from one alone.
I heard a poet sing;
And I make bold
To say 'Twould take a crowd
Of such as you
To bring me down,
I am so proud;
And if you multiply
New loves, so I.
He declared it took
Two fans in double yoke
To moider one,

Two fans, before his broke;
And three shy fans before
The man who studied war,
The Mandarin
Of T'sow gave in;
And twenty ladies to undo
The Duke of Ting,
The Lord of Lu.

ALAS!

I LOST my Love,
I lost my Love
Because she came too rich to me.
How could I dream
Her need was of
A love as rich again from me?

And now her dear,
Dark eyes light up;
Her hands caress another's hair.
For me there is
Not any hope;
But thoughts that, O,
Enrich Despair!

WOMEN

WOMEN are our subconscious selves,
Materialisations from our souls'
Regions where fairy queens and elves
Disport beyond Reason's controls.
Remember, if you call them fools

Who go, like dreams, by contraries,
That Spirits may scoff at earthly rules:
That you were born of one of these.
What else explains their vagaries
Unless this theory be truth,
That women are the Dryades
Of the lost orchards of our youth?

I WONDER

I WONDER when will women know the glories they suggest
to us:
If I were fit to sing to them of all that they inspire,
Their dalliance to open up the Kingdom of the Blest to us
Would still be no less graced than hers who had a god
to sire.

For queens they are, forgetful of the weight their brows
has belted,
No longer crowned above us all by aching diadems;
Some god put Lethe in the cup wherein the pearl was melted;
And golden heads have still to hear that Troy went
down in flames.

It surely cannot be that I, alone of men, remember
The old mad grandeur and the days of glory gone to
waste;
Because here Beauty gleams as fair as boughs rimed in
December,
And witless wears the ribbands for which helmets were
unlaced?

And yet they look as though none heard what fortresses
were wrecked for them.
What armies squandered, for a smile, the sister of all
Force;

What waters turned to wells of wine when battlements were
    decked for them:
  O why should I that Past recall which makes the Present
    worse?

It may be that our Present is for all the Past an Hades;
    A parody of Kings and Queens, and Beauty's paradigm;
It may be Time's Magnificat must name no living ladies;
    It may be that Forgetfulness excels a poet's rhyme.

THE IMAGE-MAKER

HARD is the stone, but harder still
The delicate preforming will
That, guided by a dream alone,
Subdues and moulds the hardest stone,
Making the stubborn jade release
The emblem of eternal peace.

If but the will be firmly bent,
No stuff resists the mind's intent;
The adamant abets his skill
And sternly aids the artist's will,
To clothe in perdurable pride
Beauty his transient eyes descried.

WITH A COIN FROM SYRACUSE

WHERE is the hand to trace
The contour of her face:
The nose so straight and fine
Down from the forehead's line;

Love and Beauty

The curved and curtal lip
Full in companionship
With that lip's overplus,
Proud and most sumptuous,

Which draws its curve within,
Swelling the faultless chin?
What artist knows the tech-
nique of the Doric neck:

The line that keeps with all
The features vertical,
Crowned with the thickly rolled
And corrugated gold?

The curious hands are lost
On the sweet Asian coast,
That made the coins enwrought,
(Fairer than all they bought)

With emblems round the proud
Untroubled face of god
And goddess. Or they lie
At Syracuse hard by

The Fountain Arethuse.
Therefore from Syracuse
I send this face to her,
Whose face is lovelier.

Alas, and as remote
As hers around whose throat
The curving fishes swim,
As round a fountain's brim.

It shows on the reverse
Pherenikos the horse;
And that's as it should be:
Horses she loves, for she

Is come of the old stock,
Lords of the limestone rock,
And acres fit to breed
Many a likely steed,

Straight in the back and bone,
With head high like her own,
And blood that, tamed and mild,
Can suddenly go wild.

PORTRAIT

(Diana Clothed)

Who would have thought
That your mottled and your speckled,
Wavering and dappled,
Leaf-brown costume in the light,
Held at the shoulder
By an orchid's freckled anther,
Covering a bosom of an interrupted white,
Was but the pelt
That the Maiden, the Resistless,
Light of Heel, the Huntress,
Yes; the tall Toxophilite,
Skinned in the brakes
From a slowly dying panther,
Shot in the brakes
By her fatal arrow's flight?—
Nothing to do with a merciful mild amice;—

Too well I know, and it needs no second sight!
Ah, now I know;
I should long ago have guessed it
From your way who wear it,
It is nothing more than this:
Cruelty clings to it—
It is nothing but the chlamys
Covering, and showing up
The breast of Artemis!

PERFECTION

By Perfection fooled too long,
I will dream of that no longer!
Venus, you have done me wrong
By your unattainable beauty,
Till it seemed to be my duty
To belittle all the throng.
I have found attraction stronger;
I have found a lady younger
Who can make a hard heart stir;
Like an athlete, tall and slender,
With no more than human splendour;
Yet, for all the faults of her,
Than Perfection perfecter.

Though she guards it, grace breaks through
Every blithe and careless movement.
What shall I compare her to?
When she takes the ball left-handed,
Speed and sweetness are so blended
Nothing awkward she can do,
She, whose faults are an improvement!
If she only knew what Love meant

I would not be seeking now
To describe the curbed perfection
Of all loveliness in action.
Perfect she would be, I vow,
With the mole above the brow!

PORTRAIT WITH BACKGROUND

DERVORGILLA'S supremely lovely daughter,
Recalling him, of all the Leinstermen Ri,
Him whose love and hate brought o'er the water,
    Strongbow and Henry;

Brought rigid law, the long spear and the horsemen
Riding in steel; and the rhymed, romantic, high line;
Built those square keeps on the forts of the Norsemen,
    Still on our sky-line.

I would have brought, if I saw a chance of losing
You, many more—we are living in War-rife time—
Knights of the air and the submarine men cruising,
    Trained through a life-time;

Brought the implacable hand with law-breakers,
Drilled the Too-many and broken their effrontery;
Broken the dream of the men of a few acres
    Ruling a country;

Brought the long day with its leisure and its duty,
Built once again the limestone lordly houses—
Founded on steel is the edifice of Beauty,
    All it avows is.

Here your long limbs and your golden hair affright men,
Slaves are their souls, and instinctively they hate them,
Knowing full well that such charms can but invite men,
  Heroes to mate them.

Eyes of the green of the woods that maddened Tristram!
Fair skin and smooth as the rosy-footed dove's wing!
Who would not fight, if he saw you, against this tram-
  melling of Love's wing?

Aye; and bow down, if he saw but half the vision,
I dare not call to the mind's eye, to adore you;
And be, if that great light shone with precision,
  Awe-struck before you.

TO ETHNE

I saw a beautiful face,
 And ever since the seeing,
To pause for a moment's space
 Is to bring it again into being.

Over the splendour and gloom
 Of thoughts, like a misty star,
As a goddess out of a mist would come
 To the hard-prest sons of war.

Memory, enfold her and cling!
 And I will go forth against odds.
But heart, forget her and sing!
 This is no place for the Gods.

AN APPEAL FROM THE JUDGMENT OF PARIS

STATELINESS and elegance:
But a kindness in her glance
Gives a lover heart of grace
To appraise her lovely face.
Therefore, though she may not know it,
Sings her humblest, mildest poet
Whom the thought of her makes strong
Thus to challenge with a song,
Challenge Venus' whole entourage
By the virtue of the courage
That her gracefulness engenders,
Grace, the crown of beauty's splendours.

If that young Idalian lout,
When the apple went about
Only had the rare good luck
On her loveliness to look,
What a row there would have been
For, if he had only seen
All the ecstasies and loves
That her limbs make when she moves,
Venus had not had the pippin,
Nor would he have had the strippin'
Of young Leda's swan-white daughter;
Nor had Troy gone down in slaughter.

Paris lived too soon to see
All the sights that ravish me.
I am left alone to grapple
With my love without an apple:
So I sing by her inspired,
Her whose beauty when attired

By good taste can well outdo
All that nude Idalian crew
And still hide sweets; for more, I wis,
The body than the raiment is.

GOLDEN STOCKINGS

GOLDEN stockings you had on
In the meadow where you ran;
And your little knees together
Bobbed like pippins in the weather,
When the breezes rush and fight
For those dimples of delight,
And they dance from the pursuit,
And the leaf looks like the fruit.

I have many a sight in mind
That would last if I were blind;
Many verses I could write
That would bring me many a sight.
Now I only see but one,
See you running in the sun,
And the gold-dust coming up
From the trampled butter-cup.

PRAISE

WHY should I hold my praise
To wait for better days?
The best of times is now;
And this is good enough:
For Youth is at its best,
Youngest and loveliest,
Full of the sapling stuff;
And so are you.

Praise

We shall not in the flesh
Ever again be as fresh,
With courage quite so stout.
Never shall I surprise,
Never with more delight,
The little mist of light
As if your soul shone out
Before your eyes.

Roses and snow betoken
Your words before they're spoken;
Nothing can be more small,
Nothing more fair unless
The smile that makes them glisten . . .
O bear with me and listen!
The fact remains for all
Your humbleness!

The poplar never stoops,
The gentle willow droops,
Your walk holds both of these.
The movement of your hips
Has so much buoyance in it . . .
Be silent! Just a minute . . .
It makes me think of ships
Upon far seas.

Now let me have my say
In my own lyric way;
And then you may not frown.
My song is half a ruse
To praise myself in you,
Silence would never do,
It cost a man his Muse
When Rome went down.

Love and Beauty

Never shall it be said
Of me when I am dead:
He had too tardy sense
Of Beauty.   Though your frowns
Are all my thanks, I tried
To sing of lovely pride;
There are no laurel crowns
For reticence!

A PRAYER FOR HIS LADY

If it be kindness, God, be kind
To her tall fragrant form and mind
And leave her in this world of ours
Unageing as she is in yours;
And let not Time's contagion blur
The image of your dream in her.

Little enough we have we know
Of love in Life to lead us through
And Loveliness is on the wing:
Leave the wild cherry with the Spring
In spangling showers to tremble away;
But of your grace preserve the clay.

I TREMBLE TO THINK

I TREMBLE to think that soon
Darkness shall close my sight,
And all that under the sun
I saw, and by moonlight:

Beautiful shadows and forms,
Colours, and, over the hill,
Clouds, like visible storms
At peace when the air is still;
The nameless, wonderful hues
That torture the eyes with joy
When the sea has a faint primrose,
On its blue and silver alloy—
All to be left untold,
The white and ethereal blue
That carries the chaos of gold
Dreams that I dreamt of you!
But these the years must spare,
Too transient far for time:
There is no age for the air,
Light is not of our clime.
But I whom the nets of the years
Surely at last shall enmesh
Before I can save in verse
The timeless traits of the flesh,
Shall have no peace till the cloud
Of thought takes definite shape,
And bodies you forth unbowed,
Tall, on a bare landscape,
Where earth the stone upthrusts—
Holding your exquisite frock
Against the morning gusts,
And light is on half the rock.

TO AN OLD LADY

WHERE are the eyes that remember your beauty?
Where is the lover whose lingering eyes
Remember the vision by which they were haunted,
Remember the one thing his whole being wanted,
When you took the Spring and his youth by surprise?

163

Why can we hardly imagine its blooming
When we consider a rose overblown?
Why should the mind with its outlook immortal
Join with those thoughts which dwell more on the portal
Less on the threshold of loveliness gone?

AND SO ON

WAS there ever Beauty yet
   Time forgot to counteract?
If by Sorrow unbeset,
   Did her city go unsacked;
Nor some accident disguise
The Immortals' jealousies?

Beauty never comes on earth
   But an equal Grief is born;
Hidden, maybe, in the dearth
   Of the hours ere the morn;
Or that in her core are strife,
Gain of Love and loss of Life.

This is nothing new at all:
   We have heard it all before:
Beauty one side of the Wall,
   On the other side, the War.
Love and Death; and no denying
These things do not end by dying.

LIFE AND DEATH

Life and Death

THE AIRMAN'S BREASTPLATE

(Part of the Lorica or breastplate of St. Patrick turned into rhyme at the suggestion of an Army Air Force Pilot)

I ARISE above the clouds
Armoured in the strength of God's
Presence and omnipotence
That can drive all evil hence.

I arise in Heaven's might,
In the splendour and the sight
Of the Sun; and with the ire
Of Lightning and irresistible Fire.

Stabilised upon my road,
Held up by the might of God,
With God's wisdom for my light;
Eye of God for my foresight;
Ear of God to help my hearing;
Word of God to give a bearing.

Christ before me, Christ behind me,
Christ above me, Christ below me;
Christ to be my guard abounding
Against drowning, burning, wounding:
Christ in all I do and dare:
Christ in me to win His war.

THE BUBBLE

I SAW a bubble on the water,
  A floating dome diffracting light
Into the colours of the rainbow
  Above the stones where waves were white.

I said, Too soon it must be broken
  And all its lovely world undone.
To my surprise it rose up rounded,
  A sphere of sunlight in the sun.

It may be dancing on the tree tops,
  It may be, by a light breeze, fanned
To where bright things cause little wonder:
  A meteor in Fairyland.

O wedding of the air and water,
  O child of two unstable things,
You just as well reflected sunlight
  As if you had immortal wings.

For Time itself may be unstable
  And in ourselves the fault may be
Disturbing all the sliding water,
  A rock of Immortality.

PANURGE

(Emotional Humanity, the All-worker.   A note on Rabelais)

DESIRE that drives where Lust obscures,
And Fear that wields a scourge,
  These, as the Master dreamed, are yours,
                    Panurge.

Panurge

Desire and Fear, the Masquers two,
Who act with us and urge
The Comedy we play with you,
                              Panurge.

Not since the most pellucid air
By the Illissus' verge
Heard the loud peals of laughter rare,
                              Panurge,

In lyric plenitude of joy,
Like Clouds whose rains asperge
The desiccations that destroy,
                              Panurge,

Such laughter-lore as this was taught
In which we mix and merge,
O profligate and polyglot
                              Panurge!

The meaning of the things we do:
Is Life a dance or dirge?
Depends upon the point of view,
                              Panurge!

How can we reach, though sail be bent
Beyond the horizon's verge,
Those isles of your astonishment,
                              Panurge?

Bring back the cannon's fearful crack;
Your fright and plight and purge;
The boar-cat Rodilardus, back
                              Panürge.

Bring back the fornicating Friar;
Let Sacred Strength resurge
And rehabilitate Desire,

            Panurge!

TIME, GENTLEMEN, TIME!

O WOULD not Life be charming
   Could we get rid of clocks,
The still ones and alarming
   That break on sleep with shocks?

Then it would be respected
   And worthier far of Man
Than when by springs directed
   From gold or a tin can.

Why should Man's life be reckoned
   By anything so queer
As that which splits the second
   But cannot tell the year?

If we got rid of watches
   The trains would cease to run,
We could not fight a battle-ship
   Or aim a battle gun,

Nor tune the little engines
   Which fill the towns with fumes
And send men with a vengeance
   (Quite rightly) to their tombs.

Time, Gentlemen, Time!

If we got rid of watches
    And wanted to approach
The pallid peopled cities
    We'd have to hire a coach

And guard, who, to arouse us,
    So hardy in the morn,
Outside the licensed houses
    Would blow a long bright horn.

Our stars know naught of watches,
    There's not a wind that wists
Of mischief that Time hatches
    When handcuffed to our wrists.

No wonder stars are winking,
    No wonder heaven mocks
At men who cease from drinking
    Good booze because of clocks!

'Twould make a devil chortle
    To see how all the clean
Free souls God made immortal
    Must march to a machine.

It makes me wonder whether
    In this grim pantomime
Did fiend or man first blether:
    "Time, Gentlemen, Time!"

We must throw out the timing
    That turns men into gnomes,
Of piece-work and of miming
    That fills the mental homes.

Life and Death

We must get rid of errors,
   And tallies and time checks,
And all the slavish terrors
   That turn men into wrecks.

They have not squared the circle,
   They have not cubed the sphere,
Their calendars all work ill
   Corrected by "leap" year.

But we should all be leaping
   As high as hollyhocks
Did we desist from keeping
   Our trysts with slaves of clocks.

How should we tell the seconds?
   The time a blackbird takes,
To screech across a lane-way,
   And dive into the brakes.

How should we tell the minutes?
   The time it takes to swipe
A lonely pint of Guinness,
   Or load a friendly pipe.

O make the heart Time's measure
   Because, the more it beats,
The more Life fills with pleasure,
   With songs or sturdy feats;

Our clocks our lives are cheating,
   They go, and ground we give;
The higher the heart's beating,
   The higher then we live.

CENTAURS

To get away from Reason seems
   To be the first thing one must do
To live in happiness; with dreams
   Some cloud the mind, and some bedew
The intellect with subtler juice,
   Till good Lyaeus sets them free;
Some use tobacco, some abuse
   The herbs of healing: suffer me
To live with leathery women and men
   Who give their whole mind up to horses;
Mount and dismount and mount again,
   And leave the stars to their own courses.
On through the morning air to go,
   To break the rainbow on the briar,
To hold the horse, to hear him blow
   The bellows of primaeval fire;
To feel life surging through the dark
   As waywardly as once it came
Before the filched unnatural spark
   Outshone the kindly natural flame.
Thus was the Ancient Wisdom found,
   A wisdom suited to my mind,
And taught by Chiron the renowned,
   The man and animal combined.

ANGLERS

THAT pleasant Chinese poet Ching Chih Ho,
   Who spent his time in fishing with no bait,
Recalled at last from exile, would not go,
   Nor leave the stream where he could meditate
And foil all interrupters by his ruse,
   Sitting beside the water with his line;

Was it a wonder that he should refuse,
When he could catch his rhythms half asleep,
　　Watching below the lilies fishes shine,
Or move not—it was all the same to him—
And river-mosses when he gazed more deep
And deeper, clouds across the azure swim?
　　There's not a roof now on the courts whose schemes
Kept men awake and anxious all night long,
Distracted with their working out; but dreams
He made in idleness and turned to Song
　　Can still delight his people. As for me,
I, who must daily at enactments look
　　To make men happy by legality,
Envy the poet of that baitless hook.

THE OLD GOOSE

The daylong rains are dried,
Cold is the mountain-side,
The evening light is pied,
　　Not heaven's four quarters
Know if the moon be set,
But where green sods are wet
The white stream holds you yet,
　　Lover of airs and waters!

Soon you will cross the loam,
And walk the pathway home
Before the faint stars come,
　　And seek your stable.
Your old wild life exchanged
For comfort: all is changed;
For rime-white deserts ranged,
　　A white-washed gable!

174

The Old Goose

Oh, have you quite forgot,
The flights outbreasting thought
Before this homely lot
   Half tamed your pinions?
The mountains and the stars
Were once your only bars,
And where the north wind soars
   Were your dominions.

You know the depths of air,
You know the times of year,
To you all paths are clear
   And heights of heaven,
The fens and broken bays
Where never an hunter strays;
All cold inhuman ways
   To you are even.

And all those mirrors known
That turn the mountains down:
Your flight a moment shown
   In gloaming deeper
Than those high tranquil tides
Through which your courage rides
When some straight purpose guides
   Its winged keeper.

There's blue beyond the peak
Of Patrick's frozen Reek,
Oh take on breast and beak
   The night's dark onset,
Washed in the mauve twilight
O'er some far western bight,
Where islands rest in light
   Long after sunset!

Life and Death

Islands that gleam and float
Untouched by voyaging boat,
Withheld but not remote,
   Where wave breaks slowly
Till all the beach is green,
Where the great lords are seen
Who fought and loved a Queen,
   Armed, amorous, and holy.

Easy to put life by
When friend and foe were nigh;
Easy for them to die
   Armed and elated!
And well they died in sooth,
Who found, in fighting, truth
Before old age had youth
   Repudiated.

Theirs was the exultant age,
Theirs the ecstatic rage;
And the embellished page
   Enshrined the slaying.
For, as old bards averred,
The song goes with the sword,
O wing that writ'st the Word,
   Write down this saying:

Love life and use it well:
That is the tale they tell,
Who broke it like a shell,
   And won great glory.
But you and I are both
Inglorious in sloth,
Unless our ranging youth
   Redeem our story.

For not preserved by fear
We fell on quiet here,
Our friends all dead and dear,
   A brave blithe army.
You have your grassy spring
And cloudy barrèd wing;
And I old dreams that sing,
   And memories stormy.

So that the egg be laid
For feathers unafraid,
What matter where is made,
   When strong winds tire,
The nest, if we can spend
Our age in peace, my friend?
After the journey's end
   The village spire!

NON BLANDULA ILLA

WHEN that which bore my body up takes wings
At night-fall, and my limbs are thrown to rest,
I watch in wonder, as it makes its quest,
The place it chooses for its wanderings.
No easeful meadows nor delightful springs
Nor visionary islands lure it best,
But far-off on the margin of the West
A sea-grey house whereby the blackbird sings.
The waves come up like Berserks from the sea,
The crystal mountains yield a little sand,
Through level light the bird of valour calls.
Adventurous as a Viking must that be
Which will not rest when sleep on Nature falls
But hastens to the confines of the land.

THE HO HO BIRD

My mind last night was gaily stirred
By wingings of the Ho Ho bird,
The Oriental bird that flies
Only (they say) in Paradise.
I watched its feathers trail and wing
Through air as soft as soundless Spring.
It left behind it as it came,
A path of amethystine flame;
Below, the willows slept, and bent
Their yellow heads and dreamed and leant;
A placid stream their tendrils showed;
Afar the turquoise mountains glowed
And pushed aside their mists to watch
The bird that has on earth no match.
Surely, I thought, it seems absurd
To see the landscape match the bird:
Mountains and trees and rocks and springs
Answer the waving of its wings:
When, suddenly, to my surprise,
My mind became a Paradise.

THE EMPEROR'S DREAM

When the internal dream gives out,
I let my eyes wander about
Amongst the gay and the grotesque
Ornaments upon my desk,

Where books are set on end and stacked,
By Plato and by Homer backed;
But, in the present mood preferred,
I see my Chinese crystal bird:

178

The Emperor's Dream

A Phoenix maybe, who can say?
That ship that, off Arabia,
Sighted the Phoenix flying East,
Its crew could tell about it best.

They did not need a second look;
They knew it by the course it took;
And who am I to disagree,
When China sends it back to me

To sit before me carven clear,
As if the very atmosphere
Of regions where but dreams abide,
Were seized on and solidified

To crystal that shall last as long
As Beauty gains from Art and Song,
From those who bend to carve or sing,
Their tribute to her flying wing?

Was ever artist more supreme
To catch, to hold, to mould a dream,
Year in, year out, day after day,
And never to let a line go astray

Till undistracted, undeterred,
He caught the seldom-flying bird;
From solid air he carved its crest;
And set it airy in its nest?

I send my thoughts across the skies
Of regions where the Phoenix flies,
Where Past and Present are as one,
To bow before the Emperor's throne;

179

And seek the artist in the court,
Where only such as he resort;
And from these barbarous times and ways
Offer my crude barbarian praise.

Before we meet, I shall be told
How one day in the days of old,
The Emperor hearing what he did
(For nothing's from the Emperor hid)

Commanded him to send a proof
Of what on wing or fin or hoof
He fashioned with such skill that, poor,
His name yet reached an Emperor;

And that, when he had seen the bird,
He paused, and solemnly averred:
The crystal wings without a flaw
Were those that in a dream he saw.

And how the artist with bowed head
And eyes cast down, replied and said:
That all that made for skill he owed
To Him from Whom perfection flowed.

For in the Emperor's mind were held
Art's emblems; and, if one excelled,
Of those who mould, or carve or limn,
His genius was due to him.

And that at this the Emperor laughed,
Praising the master of a craft
Which had so worthily enshrined
Things hidden in an Emperor's mind.

We need not meet, since this is so:
What every craftsman knows, we know:
Before our work stands up complete,
The Emperor must have dreamt of it.

And if we please the Emperor's whim,
And perfectly produce his dream,
Time can but turn the works of men
Into an Emperor's dream again.

LULLABY

WANDER no more, my Thoughts, but keep
Within the moated realm of Sleep;
Wander no more, nor farther than
The dusty wavering moth may span,
With wings that love the hearth-low light
With which the casement gilds the night;
     Wander no more!

Content you there to rest and dream,
Nor watch the flickering armour gleam,
For nothing that the past has done
Need break your rest to ponder on,
Nor yet the future's lordlier scope:
Sleep is a sounder thing than Hope,
     Content you there.

So yield to dream, and feel the sway
Of Earth upon the rainbow way;
And dream you feel it lift and take
A way you never felt awake;
For O, unless your dreams outdo
Your life, there is not much for you;
     So yield to dream.

On darkness launched, now you go forth
Where there is neither South or North;
Nor now and then, nor here and there;
But something deeper than these are;
So may you, when you reach that bourne,
Be most reluctant to return,
                    On darkness launched.

THE MILL AT NAUL

I CALL to mind, to bring me sleep,
That ruin on the naming hill
Of Naul, with ivy on the keep
That looks down on a ruined mill.
Because my mind comes home and rests
On things which Time no more molests:
For keep above and mill below
There is no further way to go:
They have already gone so far
With Time, that as the hill they are,
Or as the mill-pond by the mill,
Which, though it flows, is standing still;
Or as the stream and broken range
That only know immortal change;
For Time gives here, in turn for peace,
Man's handiwork a timeless lease;
And makes and takes it to its own
As if it were a stream or stone.
And that is why I love to call
To mind the drowsy mill at Naul,
Because such old things flatter me
With warrants of Eternity,
When Time's close flag suspends the fray
With ivy green against the gray.

And I can leave my pride which raged
Too long, here, in the keep besieged;
And let my love descend to spread
Through lowly roofs the gift of bread;
And know that I need range no more
With Love and Pride accounted for.

I see the mill, as day is done,
In sunset of a tardy sun
That fills the valley to the East
With all the overflowing West;
Until the valley brims to hold
An airy pond of dusty gold
That shows, as if far down in dream,
The hill, the mill, the little stream.

The light is golden down below,
But, on the keep, the afterglow
Is cold as steel, and sideways flung
Where ivy leaves the walls unhung.

I saw it first through air so wet
With dew that falling leaves fell straight;
For woods, for all their brazen towers,
Withstand not Autumn's golden showers:
So where I stood the road was rich
With bronze and gold that filled the ditch;
And boughs and leaves dropped so much rain,
I said, The wheel may turn again,
And belt itself with drops anew,
And yet not beat these woods for dew.

And now I lie till, in my mind,
The mill is lit, the keep is lined
With men-at-arms on sentry-go
Who stand to watch the mill below.

Life and Death

I see the pond's potential power
Where might is stilled to conjure flour,
And, from the strength of rain pent up
From heaven, transform an earthly crop.
I catch the mill-wheel's homely sound,
The uncouth magic of its round
Splashing bright blessings, as it turns,
On twinkling tufts and dangling ferns,
Performing, with expansive girth,
The mingling rites of heaven and earth;
I see and hear it clear as day
Though Naul is eighteen miles away.

Don't think these are the only turns
The half-unconscious mind discerns.
I see far more than you can spy
Who are not half asleep as I;

I see the way, now half awake,
The protons and electrons take
To spin the world, and bring the grist
To wild dreams of the scientist,
Who knows, for all he hopes to know,
That round a myriad mill-wheels go
From some far pond, unplumbed and still,
Which breaks to power and moves the mill.

And now I dwindle till my stream
Is lost within the pond of dream,
The pond of dream which holds far more
Than any stream of earth can pour;
But, if I lie resigned and still,
The pond at length may rise and fill.

I do not wonder that none found
The roofless mill restored and sound,

The Mill at Naul

Because the more the mind's alert
The more the inner eye is hurt,
An eye to which the light of day
Is rarely helpful, anyway.

Before I had a mind at all,
The mill was working well at Naul;
And, maybe, when I am resigned
To lose in sleep the wakeful mind,
The mill may start to work again
As once it stood to grind the grain;
And hum its song for many a season,
Where now it does not stand to reason.

It seems to me that far down there
The dusky light is dustier,
The dust is rising in the air;
And over every window square
There is an eyebrow dusty white;
And should that roof be half so bright
Unless with flour? It must be flour;
The mill is trembling into power!

And now I hear a distant drone,
The upper and the nether stone,
So far away it only comes
To fade away in waving hums,
That tell of work so sweet and strong
That all that holds it turns to song.

The mill beside the stream is lit
As if its walls were golden wheat;
And only in the upper streams
Of light a lonely sea-bird gleams
In one long arc . . . ah, let it go;
I want to watch the mill below.

Life and Death

The purple evening turns to dark,
I soon shall see the cobbles spark
Where unseen horses pull their load
Of sacks along a rising road.
I wonder if I dared look up
To see the hill, would all this stop?
And all the scenes that sleep has made,
To deeper sleep return to fade?
I wonder now, will this go on
When light, when light is quite withdrawn;
And if, when sleep is deeper still,
The mill without the Miller will?

PALINODE

TWENTY years are gone
    Down the winding road,
Years in which it shone
    More often than it snowed;
And now old Time brings on,
    Brings on the Palinode.

I have been full of mirth;
    I have been full of wine;
And I have trod the earth
    As if it all were mine;
And laughed to bring to birth
    The lighter lyric line.

Before it was too late,
    One thing I learnt and saw:
Prophets anticipate
    What Time brings round by law;
Call age before its date
    To darken Youth with awe.

Why should you drink the rue?
　　Or leave in righteous rage,
A world that will leave you
　　Howe'er you walk the stage?
Time needs no help to do
　　His miracle of age.

A few years more to flow
　　From miracle-working Time,
And surely I shall grow
　　Incapable of rhyme,
Sans Love and Song, and so
　　An echo of a mime.

Yet if my stone set forth
　　The merry Attic blade's
Remark, I shall have worth
　　Achieved before Life fades:
"A gentle man on Earth
　　And gentle 'mid the Shades."

DOMI

This is the house where I lie down
At length to call the world my own;
And no one spies on what goes on.

This is the house that cannot yield:
Who built it knew well how to build.
None trespasses across my field;

Nor comes betimes because he thought
If late, I might be up and out;
Here I am safe from fools like that.

Life and Death

The light is not as, shall we say,
The diamond dome above the Bay
When light looks black at topmost day;

Nor such as, ere the sun is set,
Shines level where the boughs are wet,
And it is early April yet.

No, I acknowledge it is dim;
But all the more tempered for him
Who has seen all that life could limn.

Before I took this holiday,
I often heard companions say:
"I would that I were well away."

And well away from all turmoil,
And well away from all the coil
Of anxious engaging toil.

Tiber and Nile and Thames of course,
Raise lordlier walls to men of force:
But this becomes a man of verse.

You must not judge by my retreat
That I found Life not wildly sweet,
Or that I turn my back to it.

'Twas pleasant as I saw it played.
But why should one whose looks grow staid
Hang on unto the harlequinade?

It needs no skill to be prepared
For the long solitude unshared:
Hither my old grandmother fared.

ELBOW ROOM

ASTRONOMERS describe a place,
Seen through a crack in the vault of Space
So dark, so absolute, so far,
No light wave from the oldest star
Nor even the thought of God can reach
And fainting fall on that far beach:
Abhorrent and inhuman this
Chineses call, "The Great Abyss."
But I am cheered, for now I know
There's somewhere left for a man to go—
(Always supposing one would care
When dead for going anywhere)
But what a place to make your goal
And lift your head and rouse your soul!
Oh! what a place to speak your mind
Without disquieting mankind!
There's where I would find elbow room
Alone beyond the crack of doom.

ALL THE PICTURES

I TOLD him he would soon be dead.
"I have seen all the pictures," said
My patient. "And I do not care."
What could a doctor do but stare
In admiration half amused
Because the fearless fellow used
"The pictures" as a metaphor,
And was the first to use it for
Life which he could no longer feel
But only see it as a reel?

189

Was he not right to be resigned
To the sad wisdom of his mind?
Who wants to live when Life's a sight
Shut from the inner senses quite;
When listless heart and cynic mind
Are closed within a callous rind;
When April with its secret green
Is felt no more but only seen;
And Summer with its dusky meadows
Is no more than a play of shadows;
And Autumn's garish oriflamme
Fades like a flickering skiagram;
And all one's friends are gone, or seem
Shadows of dream beyond a dream?
And woman's love not any mo,
Oh, surely then 'tis time to go
And join the shades that make the Show!

SUNT APUD INFERNOS TOT MILIA
FORMOSARUM

I, AS the Wise Ones held of old,
    Hold there's an Underworld to this;
And do not fear to be enrolled
    In Death's kind metamorphosis.

More wonderful than China's halls
    To Polo; more than all the West
That shone through the confining walls
    When great Magellan made the quest.

Enlarged and free, the wings of Rhyme
    Cannot outreach its purple air;
The generations of all Time
    And all the lovely Dead are there.

TO DEATH

But for your Terror
Where would be Valour?
What is Love for
   But to stand in your way?
Taker and Giver,
For all your endeavour
You leave us with more
     Than you touch with decay!

PER ITER TENEBRICOSUM

Enough! Why should a man bemoan
A Fate that leads the natural way?
Or think himself a worthier one
Than those who braved it in their day?
If only gladiators died,
Or Heroes, Death would be his pride;
But have not little maidens gone,
And Lesbia's sparrow—all alone?

MARCUS CURTIUS

*In response to an oracle which declared that a gulf recently opened in
the Forum could only be closed by casting into it that which Rome held
most dear, Marcus Curtius, fully armed, mounted his war-horse and
plunged, for that which Rome held dearest was her chivalry.*

'Tis not by brooding on delight
That men take heart of pride, and force
To pull the saddle-girthings tight
And close the gulf on staring horse.

From softness only softness comes;
Urged by a bitterer shout within,
Men of the trumpets and the drums
Seek, with appropriate discipline,

That Glory past the pit or wall
Which contradicts and stops the breath,
And with immortalising gall
Builds the most stubborn things on death.

NON DOLET

OUR friends go with us as we go
    Down the long path where Beauty wends,
Where all we love forgathers, so
    Why should we fear to join our friends?

Who would survive them to outlast
    His children; to outwear his fame—
Left when the Triumph has gone past—
    To win from Age, not Time, a name?

Then do not shudder at the knife
    That Death's indifferent hand drives home,
But with the Strivers leave the Strife,
    Nor, after Caesar, skulk in Rome.

DEATH MAY BE VERY GENTLE

DEATH may be very gentle after all:
He turns his face away from arrogant knights
Who fling themselves against him in their fights;
But to the loveliest he loves to call.
And he has with him those whose ways were mild
And beautiful; and many a little child.

ELEGIES

TO PETRONIUS ARBITER

PROCONSUL of Bithynia,
Who loved to turn the night to day,
Yet for your ease had more to show
Than others for their push and go.
Teach us to save the Spirit's expense,
And win to Fame through indolence.

BILL BAVELER

BILL BAVELER kept the Brown Stone Inn
    To serve the township and the traveller;
And many a time I would drop in,
    When noons were hot, to "see" Bill Baveler.

Somewhat below the middle size,
    Though he was short, he was not bossy;
He had large, candid, dark blue eyes
    Like his linoleum, clean and glossy.

He was too old to go to war,
    His heart was bad, he could not march hard,
He hoped he was not "steering for"—
    He'd look churchwards—"the marble orchard."

His rustic mind would entertain
    His simple guests whose minds were simple.
It took no zephyr from the brain
    To make their round cheeks "cream and dimple."

"What are those great big things with guns
    That on the enemy like hell come,
Like great big trucks, big iron ones?"
    If you said "Tanks," he'd say "You're welcome!"

His soul was sound and free from harm:
    A gentleman whose ways were gentle.
He'd take me gently by the arm
    At dawn when I was growing mental;

And guide me down the village street,
    (Because the moon was full of malice,
And each house looked the same in it)
    And say, "There is your fairy palace."

Ah, Death, you always take the best
    And Time alone makes you the leveller.
You might have taken any guest—
    You might have spared the good Bill Baveler.

When next you raid that little town
    Your victory can be but cheaper,
There's no one better left to down
    Than was The Brown Stone Tavern keeper.

FARRELL O'REILLY

You, Farrell O'Reilly, I feared as a boy
With your thin riding legs and your turned-in toes;
I feared the sharp, gimlet-like look in your eye,
Your rumbling brown beard and your pocketed nose.
Old friend of my Father what brings you back now?
You died fifty-nine years or sixty ago.

They say, when a man is about to be drowned,
His youth flashes back and he sees his life clear;
So, maybe, because I am nearing the ground
The days of my youth and my childhood are here.

Farrell O'Reilly

If so, they are welcome if they compensate
For days that are yearly increasing in weight.

My Father no sooner would talk of Kilbeg
And carefully measure the charge for each cartridge,
Than I saw myself strutting behind with the bag
And heard the men talk as they walked up the partridge.
The coveys were scarce, and the cause of the trouble
Was "Farrell O'Reilly's too proud to have stubble."

O thick-sodded fields that have fattened the herds
From the days of the kings in the dawn of our time,
O fields of Moynalty, The Plain of the Birds,
None ever drew plough through your land on the lime!
King Leary of Tara just over the way
Knew more about Meath than the men of to-day.

My young eyes were good and rejoiced at the sight
Of a drake with the sun all a blaze on his green
That flew on a sudden from left to the right:
What banging! But only a feather was seen.
When each man exclaimed to the other, "Bad luck!"
I could not help thinking 'twas good for the duck.

Remote as the days in an old mezzotint
When Farrell O'Reilly would lean to his gun
Top-hatted; and aim with a vigilant squint,
(If he missed, it was due to the wind or the sun)
My Father stands clear; but I see clearer Farrell
His left eye shut tight and his hand up the barrel.

In spite of their failure, I gaped at the men,
Their failures were feats to me looking for wonder.
How little I doubted Authority then!
Authority added distinction to blunder.
They could not do wrong, though they played ducks and
    drakes,
For great men can lend a prestige to mistakes.

"Now hand me that bag, for you can't lift a leg."
I said, "It's so light I can carry it farther"—
A thousand wide acres surrounded Kilbeg—
And Farrell said nothing, but looked at my Father;
Then carried me home; and I found, for a truth,
There's sometimes great kindness behind the uncouth.

The little pine wood with its floor of dense laurels;
The river slow-moving with bulrushes rimmed;
The well-house, the lis—all the things that were Farrell's,
Though half were forbidden, are shining undimmed:
The harness room filled with bits, saddles and bridles,
A room where the dairy maid gossips and idles.

I feel the lull now that came over the men,
And I see the groom wafting his smoke with his hand,
Intent as his polishing started again;
"The Master!"   A hint that they all understand;
The dairy maid holding her blouse at her throat,
As he enters the yard in his cut-away coat.

Like everyone else who was in his employ,
Alert, lest, surprised, I be taken in error,
In spite of foreboding, I snatched at my joy,
For joy is a pleasance surrounded by terror.
Wood, river and well—to maid and to man
Sharp Farrell O'Reilly appeared as god Pan.

Wood, river and well—the wild things of the fields;
The lis with its lonely and wind-twisted thorn,
Enchanted me early; now everything yields
To the breath I drew first from the winds of my morn:
So, Farrell O'Reilly, in token from me,
Accept this wild leaf from your own twisted tree.

"AETERNAE LUCIS REDDITOR"

(To Robert Yelverton Tyrrell, Professor of Classics, T.C.D.)

OLD friend, long dead, who yet can thrive
More in my heart than men alive
Because in you the flame lived more
Than ever since the days of yore
When, everywhere that Rome was known,
The post-triumphal silence shone,
And in the vespertinal hush
The trumpet yielded to the thrush:
Because those days you could restore:
Aeternae lucis Redditor.

You shared with us the mood serene
That ruled the universal scene
When Peace was guardian of the poor,
And only rusty was the door
Of Janus, and the pillared shade
Revealed the studious colonnade:
The toga with the purple hem,
The temple that with quiet flame
Acclaimed the distant Emperor,
Aeternae lucis Redditor.

Too seldom on this world of ours
Unwrackt the eternal radiance pours.
Again we shall not see it pour
As in the days and nights before
We lost the wide Virgilian calm;
Days when we sought to earn the palm—
Through the endowment of a wit
Which made us eligible for it—
From you who were Wit's arbiter,
Aeternae lucis Redditor.

'Twixt you and me and me and those
Irremeable the River flows
Since we beheld with joy and awe
The light by which blind Homer saw.
And not again in this our time
Shall sound magnanimous the rhyme;
The wolves have torn our pleasant folds,
And the Great Wall no longer holds.
But Love can bridge the Stygian shore,
Aeternae lucis Redditor.

ELEGY ON THE ARCHPOET
WILLIAM BUTLER YEATS LATELY DEAD

Now that you are a Song
And your life has come to an end
And you wholly belong
To the world of Art, my friend,
Take, for well it is due,
This tribute of my rhymes
With mind unswerved from you
In these enormous times;
Not that I wish to intrude
To mix with mine your leaf,
But that I would entwine
In your magnificent sheaf,
After sad interlude,
A spray cut from that fine
And rare plant, Gratitude.
For anything I owe
In the art of making songs
Largely to you is due,
To you the credit belongs
Who never stinted or spared

Yourself in the difficult feat
Of getting a man prepared
To sing in his own conceit.
None may carry a stone
To your high tower of thought
But surely I can own
Whose was the influence caught
Me in wild wear disguised
And undistinguished found me,
Encouraged, authorised
And with the laurel crowned me; [1]
And make it lovingly clear
While memory is fresh
What manner of man you were
While here clothed on with flesh.
The world knows well your rhymes,
But I would depict you to please
The men in coming times
By a picture of you in these
And make them as grateful to me
As I would be could I find,
Searching past history,
Troubled Euripides
Or unvexed Sophocles,
By some contemporary mind.

II

The noble head held high,
The nose with an eagle's gaze,
The sharp appraising eye,
The brown unageing face,
The beautiful elegant hands
As white as the breasts of the love
Of Ossian in faerylands:
Among us but ever aloof,

He never hurried or ran,
With eyes on a lordly track
A tall upstanding man
You dared not slap on the back.
He moved in a diffident way
As if a new-comer to earth
Wrapped in a magical day
Older than death or than birth:
A man come down from the men
Who walked in the morning dew
Of dark Ferdia's strain
With lips like berries of yew:
A race that hosts in the hills,
A race few eyes can see,
A race that our day fills
With perverse, mischievous glee:
A head never turned by fame,
An eerie spirit that takes
Its preternatural calm
From sloe-black mountain lakes.
You heard the sound of his soul
Through words in their equipoise;
The sound of his soul was beautiful:
He had a most beautiful voice.

III

O brain that never lacked full power,
O spirit always of the tower [2]
That never stooped to earthly lure
But at your height were self-secure:
With wistful child's benignity,
With Man's most noble dignity
You never compromised with fear
You brought the Brave among us here,
And high above the tinsel scene

Strode with the old heroic mien,
And equalled to your intellect
The grandeur of your self-respect.

IV

O happy were your days on earth
When we sat by the household hearth
And, as the Autumn glow went out,
Bandied the whole bright world about,
Making Reality betray
The edges of sincerer day;
Or in that orchard house of mine,—
The firelight glancing in the wine
Or on your ring that Dulac made—
How merrily your fancy played
With the lost egg that Leda laid,
The lost, third egg, Herodotos
In Sparta said he came across;
Or broached a problem more absurd:
In the Beginning was the Word,
Since there was none to hear, unheard?
Or linking stranger mysteries,
The Spring with dates of the decease
Of Caesar, Christ and Socrates,
You let imagination range
Into the fabulous and strange
Realms of the mind where, at its source,
Life is exultant and perverse.
Then presently you would recite
The verses you made overnight,
Affirming that a song should be
Bone-bare in its simplicity.
Exemplifying this, you chose
Before the Adonais, those
Straight lines of Burns on Captain Grose

"No, no! on Henderson, not Grose":
"For Matthew was a queer man";
Preferring the heartfelt, sincere,
Artless humanity of "queer"
To Shelley's cosmic sermon.
Sometimes you brought invective down
Upon the "blind and ignorant town"
Which I would half disclaim;
For in my laughing heart I knew
Its scheming and demeaning crew
Was useful as the opposite to
The mood that leads to fame;
For very helpful is the town
Where we by contradicting come
Much nearer to our native home;
But yet it made me grieve
To think its mounted-beggar race
Makes Dublin the most famous place
For famous men to leave:
Where City Fathers staged a farce
And honoured one who owned a horse; [3]
They win right well our sneers
Who of their son took no account
Though he had Pegasus to mount
And rode two hemispheres.
Return Dean Swift, and elevate
Our townsmen to the equine state!

v

Now you are gone beyond the glow
As muted as a world of snow;
And I am left amid the scene
Where April comes new-drenched in green,
To watch the budding·trees that grow
And cast, where quiet waters flow,

Their hueless patterns below;
And think upon the clear bright rill
That lulled your garden on the hill;
And wonder when shall I be made
Like you, beyond the stream, a shade.

VI

We might as well just save our breath,
There's not a good word to be said for Death
Except for the great change it brings:
For who could bear the loveliest Springs
Touched by the thought that he must keep
A watch eternal without sleep?
But yet within the ends
Of human, not eternal things,
We all resent the change it brings:
Chiefly the loss of friends:
Tyrrell, Mahaffy and Macran,
The last the gentlest gentleman,
And golden Russell—all were gone,
Still I could turn to you alone.
Now you have turned away
Into the land of sleep or dreams
(If dreams you rule them yet meseems).
With clowns in tragedy,
Here solitary, I, bereft
Of all impulse of praise, am left
Without authority or deft
Example in a rhyme.
There never was a poet yet
Could put another more in debt.
England's great-hearted Laureate [4]
Is here to testify to that
As, more indebted, I
Whose hand you held, whose line you filled,

Whose mind with reverence instilled
For the most noble and august
Art that can shake men more than lust.
Here I must bide my time
And, through my loss, grow more content
To go the way the Master went
And follow on a friend
Praising the life by art imbued,
The Apollonian attitude
And lips that murmured metre till the end.[5]

NOTES TO THE ELEGY ON WILLIAM BUTLER YEATS

[1] The Irish Academy of Letters, founded by W. B. Yeats and G. B. Shaw, crowned the author's book, WILD APPLES, some years ago.

[2] "Of the tower" is a term derived from falconry. It meant a hawk at the top of his flight and ready to stoop.

[3] Boss Croker, after his Tammany career, resided in Ireland and won the Derby with a horse bred in Ireland called *Orby*. The City Fathers gave Boss Croker the *Freedom of the City* but refused the author's suggestion that they give a similar honour to Yeats.

[4] In a memoir written shortly after Yeats's death, John Masefield, the English Poet Laureate, referred to him as: "him to whom I owe all."

[5] Lady Dorothy Wellesley in her book, *Letters on Poetry from W. B. Yeats to Dorothy Wellesley*, tells how when unconscious, dying, his lips still murmured rhyme.

LIST OF POEMS

List of Poems

INDEX OF FIRST LINES

209

Index of First Lines

Index of First Lines

Index of First Lines